MW00856160

The Greatest of These is Love:

The Life of St. Elizabeth of Hungary

by

Lori Pieper, SFO

2nd Revised Edition

NEW YORK

TAU CROSS BOOKS AND MEDIA

2013

Library of Congress Control No: 2014918241

ISBN: 978-0-9796688-5-2 (paperback)
ISBN: 978-0-9796688-6-9 (Kindle/mobi)
ISBN: 978-0-9796688-7-6 (EPUB)

Cover design by Lori Pieper

Cover Illustration: M. Perazzi, *The Charity of St. Elizabeth of Hungary (*ca. 1900); Curia Generale of the Third Order Regular of St. Francis, Basilica of Sts. Cosmas and Damian, Rome. Used with permission of the friars of the TOR.

∂

Acknowledgements

I owe a debt of gratitude to far too many people to be able to thank them all for their help with this book, but there are some above all I must mention.

I want to thank my professors at Fordham University, especially Dr. Richard Gyug, who directed my dissertation and aided my studies on St. Elizabeth.

I also want to thank the Third Order Regular friars who, out of love for Elizabeth, their patron saint, offered me their help in so many ways: Father Fernando Scocca, for permission to use the prayer on p. 167; Fr. Ilija Zivkovic, who gave me permission to use the illustration of St. Elizabeth on the cover; Fr. Michael Higgins, who helped with the technical details of the image; and Fr. Lino Temperini, who graciously made copies of his own works available to me.

I am very grateful to Bill Kalush, director of the Conjuring Arts Research Center, who provided the facilities for designing the book.

I also want to thank my brothers and sisters in the SFO, above all Barbara O'Neill, Minister of the Tau Cross Region, who offered her help and advice, and Carmel Cassidy, Minister of my own Mother of God Fraternity, who took on many of my duties as fraternity secretary while I was writing.

Special thanks to my dear friend Kenlynne Rini, who - helped proofread the book and offered invaluable moral support.

Most of all, I want to thank my parents, John and Betty Pieper, who have always believed in me.

Contents

Foreword to the Revised Edition

St. Elizabeth of Hungary (1207-1231) has a unique appeal for Christians in our troubled age. Love, rather than ideology or politics, was the basis of her whole life.

Today our world is filled with the bitterness caused by competing ideologies and the unyielding arrogance of many of those who hold them. We are also familiar with the way that treating Christian doctrine merely as a set of propositions rather than as part of a living relationship with God has lead to many distortions of the faith.

Elizabeth was a happily married woman who loved her husband and children. She was a lover not just of social justice in the abstract, but of the poor as individuals. She was a lover of God above all; we sometimes forget that no Christian teaching makes sense apart from the fact that we are made to know, and therefore to love God. Elizabeth hungered for God and found him in the everyday activities of a noblewoman, ruler, wife and mother living in the world before she found him in religious life in imitation of St. Francis. She lived contemplative prayer in the world, where a thousand daily tasks demanded her attention.

These are the aspects of Elizabeth's life that attracted me to her when I first read about her as a girl of eleven. Her example inspired me as I became a member of the Secular Franciscan Order, where we honor her as our patron. It led me ultimately to research her life as a scholar and to write my doctoral dissertation on the sources for her life.

When I was asked by my order to work on the formation program for the eighth centenary of Elizabeth's birth—a celebration due to extend from November 2006 to November 2008—I realized that no book in English for the ordinary reader would be out in time to serve as supplementary material. So I set out to write a short booklet that would speak about Elizabeth as a real woman relevant to us today, a work intended not just for the SFO, but for other Catholics and other Christians as well. But it soon became clear that something much more substantial was needed.

Since the publication of the last major English-language biographies of Elizabeth some fifty years ago, more research had been done into the sources, new sources had been uncovered, and revised interpretations of them had provided new insights into her and her world. I decided to write a book that would take into account this scholarly work, some of which I participated in myself. My short treatment could not be more than an outline, but it would be up to date.

Along with it I also presented the first English translation in more than fifty years of the documents from Elizabeth's canonization process. These include the letter by her confessor, Conrad of Marburg, and the depositions of the four women who knew her best, "Elizabeth's Four Evangelists," as they have been called.[1] I followed these traditional sources with the lost portions of her canonization process I had recently recovered from the Anonymous Franciscan.

These words of the eyewitnesses, translated in that book for the first time, are more eloquent than any summary of them could ever be. They convey not only Elizabeth's holiness but her captivating personality, and lead people who read them to feel as though they have come to know her. In particular, the new testimonies give us a clearer idea of how she lived the Franciscan life of penance. The bull of canonization gives us the first official theological reflection on Elizabeth, by Pope Gregory IX. The book concluded with some prayers, litanies and scriptural passages suitable for the celebration of her centenary.

In this new edition, I have revised and expanded the text somewhat and corrected a number of errors that were due to having to write in so short an amount of time. I hope to produce a more expanded edition in the future.

My hope is that readers will carry away from this book that love of God that led St. Elizabeth to do so much good in the world – and that they will "go and do likewise" (Lk 10:37).

Lori Pieper, OFS

November 17, 2013
Feast of St. Elizabeth

ॐ

A Note on the Sources

We are fortunate to have a number of sources for Elizabeth's life written by her contemporaries. The most important are the documents of her canonization process, composed between 1232 and 1235. These include a letter to the Pope by her confessor, Conrad of Marburg, and the depositions of four women close to her: Guda and Isentrude, who had been noble ladies of her retinue at court, and Irmingard and Elisabeth, women of humble birth who served with her at her hospital in Marburg. There are two versions of the testimonies, one shorter, one longer. The full title given to the shorter is the *Dicta quatuor ancillarum Sancte Elisabeth*, or the "Statements of the Four Handmaids of St. Elizabeth." The longer is known as the *Libellus*. There has been much discussion about these two works. It is now accepted that neither version is identical with the original depositions of the witnesses. The *Dicta* seems to be a selection from the testimonies made into a continuous narrative in rough chronological order. The *Libellus* is based on the *Dicta*, with a number of additions from unknown sources.

The other most trustworthy thirteenth-century sources are: the life of Elizabeth's husband, Ludwig IV, written by his chaplain Berthold around 1228, and contained in the chronicle written by the monks of the monastery of Reinhardsbrunn in Thuringia; the life of Elizabeth by the Cistercian monk Caesarius of Heisterbach, written in 1236-37; and the life completed in 1297 by Dominican friar Dietrich of Apolda.[1]

There is also the Anonymous Franciscan life of Elizabeth, named for its author, an unknown Friar Minor. It dates from the end of the thirteenth or very beginning of the fourteenth century.

Historians have long known about this life from fragments that survived, but often dismissed it as unreliable legend. When the complete text was discovered in 1996 in a manuscript in Trier, it turned out to contain the testimonies of a number of witnesses from Elizabeth's canonization process that are not found in the *Dicta*. This tremendous discovery adds much to our knowledge of the saint. In fact, the whole work is a treasure trove of information about the relationship between Elizabeth and the Franciscans. An edition of the complete text was published in 2000.[2]

Other Franciscan tradition on Elizabeth has been preserved, including a passage in the chronicle written by Brother Giordano of Giano about 1262, describing the establishment of the Friars Minor in Germany. There are other scattered references to Elizabeth in Franciscan sources that have never been sufficiently studied. One of the most interesting of these can be found in the *Chronicle of the Twenty-Four Generals of the Order of Minors*, written about 1374 by Arnaud de Serrant. The passage about Elizabeth is especially intriguing because it is almost entirely original, and it also contains memories of her that, like those in the Anonymous Franciscan, appear to go back to the friars who knew her.

In the first edition, partly for lack of time, and partly because I wanted to keep the book as free from cumbersome footnotes as possible, I only cited sources in notes when it was inconvenient to refer to an author or source in the text. Since the whole of Conrad's letter and the *Dicta* are translated in Part II of this book, along with the most important of the testimonies in the Anonymous Franciscan and the bull of canonization by Pope Gregory IX, I usually did not give specific footnotes to those sources. Detailed citing of the printed editions of the sources in every case would have been of little use to most English-speaking readers, because the texts themselves existed only in hard-to-find Latin editions.

This problem has now been remedied in part by the publication of an English translation by Kenneth Wolf of all the important documents from St. Elizabeth's canonization process, excluding the those from the Anonymous Franciscan, in *The Life and Afterlife of St. Elizabeth of Hungary* (New York: Oxford University Press, 2010). In this edition, I have added citations to this work where appropriate, as well as more references to the early sources, in anticipation of future English editions of them.

I have added a few explanatory notes as well for important or controversial points, in order not to interrupt the flow of the story.

Part I:

Elizabeth's Life

❧

Prologue: A Turbulent World

There are many similarities between Elizabeth's time and ours that make her life especially relevant today. She lived in the thirteenth century, the high point of the Middle Ages, a time when, after surviving many invasions and disasters, people's thoughts were turning to building up society in the world, achieving material prosperity and taking pride in secular accomplishments. At the same time, many people were becoming dissatisfied with the prevailing materialism and searching for true spiritual wealth. It was also a time when many men were leaving to fight in a controversial war in the Middle East in lands under Muslim control. Elizabeth would lose her husband because of that war.

She also lived in an age when lay spirituality was being discovered. In the early Middle Ages, monastic life was considered the main, almost the only, model of spirituality. But now lay people became aware that they too were called to holiness, and that secular occupations could be consecrated to God. Dante, the famous Italian poet, born just over thirty years after Elizabeth's death, devoted all his talents to God as a writer. He said: "Those who turn to religion are not just those who in their dress and form of life make themselves similar to St. Benedict, St. Augustine, St. Francis or St. Dominic; even those who are still in the married state can devote themselves to a good and true religious life, for the way God wants us to be religious is in our hearts."[1]

Women in Elizabeth's day, as in ours, wanted to make their voices heard in a male-dominated society. And in part they succeeded: they were no longer confined to the hearth, but were active in town guilds and religious fraternities. They also showed that they had a valuable contribution to make to the Church as well. Many women like St. Clare and St. Elizabeth sought a life of evangelical poverty beside the men in the early Franciscan movement.

Earlier spirituality had concentrated on God's majesty and his distance from all human comprehension. Thirteenth-century spirituality began to concentrate more on the earthly life of Jesus and imitation of him. This was often reflected vividly in the art of the time. The earlier Byzantine paintings, which showed Christ erect and with open eyes, triumphant on the Cross, were replaced by crucifixions that showed Jesus actually suffering. We think nothing of this now, but it was truly revolutionary to those who saw it for the first time. In Elizabeth's lifetime, St. Francis presented a living tableau of the birth of Christ in Greccio. The Virgin Mary was now represented in art not only as the Queen of Heaven, but as a mother other mothers could identify with.

The world was being transformed from a feudal economy, based on the land and agriculture, to a money economy based on commerce and trade in the towns. The peasants or serfs who lived on the lord's lands often suffered from the heavy taxation that financed his wars of expansion as Europe's large territorial states were formed. The townspeople who grew wealthy on banking and credit faced resentment from poor borrowers who suffered from heavy interest rates, which the Church condemned as usury. Fringe religious groups abounded. There were the Cathars, who denounced the corrupt clergy and the authority of the Church, and sought a "purified" religion, one which in reality did little more than reproduce ancient Gnostic heresies. They believed that the material, physical world, particularly the human body, was evil, and condemned reproductive sex for bringing more evil into the world.

The Poor of Lyon began as earnest reformers; their leaders translated the Bible into the vernacular, which was spread by both men and women preachers, and they lived poor and austere lives; but they eventually insisted on adhering to their own doctrines and would not accept the authority of the Church.

This was Elizabeth's social and spiritual world, and we recognize many of its conflicts as similar to our own. But her life as a Christian and a saint was also part of the turbulent dynastic history of Europe in her time. Elizabeth was born not much more than 200 years after her father's people first accepted Christianity. The dynasty she was born into, the Árpáds, was named after one of the six main chieftains of the pagan Magyars, Árpád, who died around 900.

His descendant Geza began to form a unified Hungarian state out of the Magyar tribes, not without a few wars and assassinations.

Geza's son Vajk (975-1038) was baptized a Christian at the age of ten with the name of Stephen. He was crowned as Hungary's first king in 1000. He had a tremendous love for the poor; he would often disguise himself as a peasant when he traveled, and carried a special purse so he could give alms to all the poor people he met. He was canonized in 1083. His son Emeric (1007-1031), is also regarded as a saint. Elizabeth's father András (or Andrew) II, was their descendant. His mother was Anne, daughter of Constance of France and Rénaud de Chatillon, the Prince of Antioch.

Elizabeth was also of German ancestry: her mother was Gertrude (1185-1213), daughter of Berthold IV, the duke of

Meran, on what is now the seacoast of Dalmatia and Istria. The family were originally the counts of Andechs in Bavaria. Elizabeth's aunt Hedwig (1174-1243), her mother's sister, who was married to Henry, the Duke of Silesia, was later declared a saint.

Andrew II and his wife Gertrude were an ambitious couple. They were married sometime before 1203, when Gertrude was not yet eighteen. Andrew had been engaged in a long struggle for the throne with his older brother Emeric. After Emeric's death, Andrew was named regent for his brother's young son, Ladislaus, but continued his intrigues against the boy's mother Constance. Gertrude supported him in his struggle. On young Ladislaus' death, Andrew ascended to the throne in 1205, at the age of 30. For all his political ruthlessness, Andrew was courteous and knightly in character, known for his piety, good nature and generosity, but also restless and volatile, with dreams of grandeur. Gertrude's constant support for her husband's plans showed her to be a woman of unusual vigor.

Elizabeth came into the world in 1207, bearing in her veins the combined blood of a newly converted people and the ancient Christian stock of Europe. She had an abundance of holy ancestors to imitate, and other ancestors who were immersed in war, political intrigues, betrayals and violence. She came into a rapidly transforming world where many people were seeking a renewal of their faith.

Some months before Elizabeth's birth, a young man in Italy, the son of a rich merchant, who had experienced the impact of the violence and greed of his time and the emptiness of soul they brought, knelt in an abandoned church to pray before the crucifix, asking for enlightenment. It seemed to him that Jesus himself spoke to him from the Cross. "Go, rebuild my Church, which you see is falling into ruin."[2] The young man was Francesco di Pietro di Bernardone of Assisi, whose life was to be bound up with Elizabeth's. Though they never met, they were partners in the rebuilding of the Church and the world in their time.

I. From Hungary to Germany

In 1207, Andrew II was fighting near the northeast borders of his territory to subdue the land conquered by his father in Galicia, or Halych-Volhynia, in what is now Poland and Ukraine.

Gertrude, as always, would have been with him. So it was in the royal fortress in Sárospatak, in northeast Hungary on the Bodrog river, that Elizabeth was most likely born.[1] The actual date of her birth is unknown, but is traditionally said to be July 7.

Elizabeth, in Hungarian Erzsébet, joined her older sister Anna Maria, born in 1203, and her brother Béla, heir to his father's throne, born in 1206. Andrew and Gertrude would later have two other children, Kálmán and András.

The Romanesque fortress at Sarospatak had been built by her father; unfortunately only a few traces of it remain. For a real sense of how Elizabeth lived her earliest years with her family, we can visit the royal palace at Esztergom, parts of which are still preserved as they were in her time. It is here that the family spent a good part of the year, for the administrative and legislative part of her father's government was carried on in this city.

The stone walls of the castle's rooms are vaulted in Romanesque style, their windows looking out over the Danube. The beautiful chapel, in the new style known as Gothic, with its soaring pointed arches, had been built by her grandfather Bela III just a few years before. This was where Elizabeth first went to Mass, and first became acquainted with the mysteries of God.

Very little has been transmitted to us about Elizabeth's early childhood. Her mother Gertrude would have been in charge of her education; because of her family origin, she would have been able to teach her German as well as Hungarian from her earliest years.

Franciscan writers of the thirteenth century record the first story about Elizabeth's love of the poor. They say that she used to go to the royal kitchens and sneak out food to give to the beggars before the castle. The kitchen workers complained about these little thefts and King Andrew heard about it. One day, he met his daughter as she was hurrying to the castle entrance with some food in the folds of her skirt. He asked what she was carrying. Frightened, the child, who was at most four years old, said, "some roses." Her father knew that it was not the season for roses, so he asked to see them; she unwrapped the bread, and it had indeed turned into roses. From then on, the king gave his daughter permission to give to the poor as much as she wanted.[2] It is a legend, of course, but one that reflects what we know of her later character. Only later did medieval writers place the incident during her marriage and have her encounter her husband, who supposedly did not want her to engage in such charitable works. The legend, while beautiful, has no place in the later period of Elizabeth's life, for her husband never opposed her giving to the poor. The attitudes of the characters in the story are actually much more in accordance with a child and a parent than a husband and wife.

Though as a king Andrew was not overburdened with foresight, he would be fortunate when it came to giving Elizabeth to the right husband. In 1211, when she was only four years old, he betrothed her to Ludwig IV, the future Landgraf of Thuringia,[3] who was then just eleven.

Ludwig's father, Landgraf Hermann I, belonged to the Ludowinger, a family that had long ruled Thuringia in central Germany, and had possessed the title of Landgraf (similar in rank to a count or duke) since 1130. He was related to the line of the Holy Roman Emperors through the marriage of his father, Louis II, known as "the Iron Landgraf," to Jutta, the half-sister of Emperor Frederick Barbarossa.

In 1211, Hermann was 55 years old. He and his second wife Sophia von Wittelsbach, daughter of Otto, Duke of Bavaria, already had six children: Irmingard, the oldest, born in 1296, Ludwig, born in 1200, Hermann, born around 1201, followed by two more sons, Heinrich Raspe and Conrad, and a daughter Agnes.

Germany was divided into little states, each governed by its own feudal ruler, whether prince, Landgraf or Markgraf (marquis). But each was a vassal of the emperor, and each had pledged loyalty to him and would fight for him when needed.

Hermann I was a turbulent ruler. Changes in the empire had recently taken place that affected his fortunes. Frederick Barbarossa's son and Hermann's cousin, Emperor Henry VI, had died in 1197, leaving a three-year-old son named Frederick. But the child was too young to govern, and the German princes jockeyed for position hoping to become the new emperor. The leading contenders were Philip of Swabia, Henry VI's brother, and Otto of Brunswick, the nephew of Richard the Lionhearted of England. Each of the rulers of the German states supported one or the other of these candidates.

In spite of his close relationship to Philip's family, Hermann initially threw his support to Otto of Brunswick. But Hermann quarreled with Otto, and soon began favoring Philip. But after Pope Innocent III had made peace between Hermann and Otto, Hermann changed sides yet again, and Philip, tired of his vacillating, invaded Thuringia and soon devastated the land.

This was only the beginning of Hermann's political troubles. The rivalry between the would-be emperors would lead to more wars and invasions. The young Frederick finally came of age in 1211, and the princes gave him their allegiance, but not before the wars had done great damage to Hermann's territories.

But Hermann did have one strong supporter who remained with him throughout his wars—King Ottokar of Bohemia. Ottokar's wife Constance was the sister of Andrew II of Hungary. Hermann's treasury was now exhausted by war, and King Andrew was rich.

An alliance with the Hungarian king and with Ottokar through the marriage of his oldest son with Andrew's daughter Elizabeth seemed like the perfect plan. It would not only fatten his treasury, but would be very useful politically: a strong league of Christian princes in the area was needed to defend their lands against the pagan tribes to the east, including the Cumins and the Tartars. For their part, Andrew and Gertrude were happy at the thought of an alliance with a family so closely related to the Emperor.

It seems shocking to us, but marriages of this kind between young children were frequent; they were political alliances, not personal decisions by the two children who were the parties most concerned. No one would have thought of consulting them, but certainly the parents still hoped that their children would be happy.

It was often the custom for the bride to be taken to the court of her future husband at a very young age, so that she could be brought up to speak the language of her new homeland and understand its customs. Hermann and Sophia sent a delegation to Hungary to bring little Elizabeth to Germany. It was made up of Count Meinhart of Mühlberg, a knight named Walther of Vargila, and Lady Bertha, the widow of Egilolf von Bendeleiben. They and their large retinue were well-armed, for they would have to travel through dangerous territory on their way eastward to Prague, Bohemia, Moravia, and the Danube. The two parties met at Poszony, a fortress on the western edge of Andrew's territories, probably so that the German delegation would not have so far to travel. They were welcomed with great ceremony.

The four-year-old princess was dressed in silk garments trimmed in silver and gold. Elizabeth's dowry was 1,000 marks in silver, a princely sum, accompanied by an abundance of gold and silver jewels for her use, and even a silver cradle. There were equally sumptuous gifts for the delegation, who in turn offered gifts to King Andrew's treasury. Gertrude sent word through the delegation to Landgraf Hermann: "Tell your lord to be patient and strong. If God lets me live, I will heap up for him still greater riches."[4] This promise was later to play a critical role in the question of Elizabeth's marriage.

Then came the time for the king and queen to say farewell to their daughter. King Andrew put Elizabeth in Walther of Vargila's arms, and said, "To your honor as a knight I entrust my supreme consolation." Walther replied. "I will protect her and always be faithful to her." At least so we are told by the author of a fourteenth-century legend of St. Elizabeth called the *Passional*.[5] He may be correct, for other sources indicate that Walther always looked on Elizabeth as his special charge. Two Hungarian priests named Farkas and David went with her to her new homeland to see to her education.

The trip back to Germany in the caravan of sumptuously loaded wagons must have seemed very exciting to the little girl. They traveled slowly, making no more than 35 to 40 miles a day. The mountains, rivers and villages they passed would have provided Elizabeth with some impressive life-long memories.

Then one day, looking over the top of the wagon, Elizabeth got her first look at her future home: Wartburg castle, on a high cliff above the town of Eisenach. The gleaming stone walls, with their arcades of round Romanesque arches, were visible to the traveler from a long way off.

Waiting for her there were the Landgraf's family. If Elizabeth was homesick, if she was frightened by the commotion of her welcoming and the strange faces of her new family, she would have been trained not to show it in public; her father and mother's teaching would have always stressed that courage must accompany noble blood.

Also waiting to welcome her was her betrothed, Ludwig, a boy of eleven. No one recorded what the two felt when they first saw each other. But that first night, according to custom, Elizabeth was put in bed with Ludwig as a symbolic pledge of their future marriage. I like to think that it was at the beginning with them as it was to be later on: that Ludwig took on himself the role of comforter.

II. Elizabeth's Childhood

From that time on, Elizabeth's life was to be divided between the older feudal world of the castle and the new urban life represented by the town of Eisenach, which had grown into a prosperous commercial center. The Landgraf leaned heavily on the towns for financial support, and his family took part in the life of the town parishes.

But the Wartburg was still the center of their lives. It had originally been built around 1080 by Hermann's ancestor, Count Ludwig the Salian, on the top of a mountain covered with birch and firs, overlooking a vast stretch of territory, a perfect spot for a defensive fortress at what was then his country's border. The first castle, consisting of a surrounding wall, a tower and a few other buildings, was inhabited by one of the Landgraf's officials.

But when Hesse was annexed to Thuringia in 1180, the Wartburg stood at the center of the Landgraf's territory, and became the family's main residence. Landgraf Ludwig III (The Pious), Hermann's brother, made it into a stately Romanesque castle. It was approached by a drawbridge. Once past the main entrance, the visitor entered the courtyard, which contained the chapel, stable, kitchen and lodgings for the captain and his men. Inside the main arcaded building were the living quarters for the Landgraf and his family. The ground floor contained a room to lodge the knights who were guests, as well as a dining hall. The *kemenate,* or room with the hearth, on the same floor, was the center of daily life for the women and children. The Landgraf took his meals with the family there when he was not traveling or on a military campaign.

The Landgraf's room and the *Sangersaal,* or singer's hall, were on the first floor. The top floor contained the feasting hall.

Elizabeth lived her life as a child in this castle; her playmates were Ludwig's sister Agnes and the daughters of the nobility assigned to her as her retinue. Her best friend was Guda, who was just a year older than she was. They played all the normal childhood games in the castle and courtyard: tag and races and follow the leader.

But Elizabeth very early became aware of something more fascinating than games. It was her secret and she tried to hide it as much as possible. Not because she was ashamed, but because it was something too big to speak about. She was fascinated by the chapel of the castle and would find every excuse she could, even while playing a game, to enter and genuflect before the altar. She was already being drawn by the presence of God she felt there.

She used every subterfuge she could, as Guda later recalled. She would race one of the girls toward the chapel, so she could enter it.

When they played follow-the-leader, she would always hop on one foot toward the chapel and jump over the threshold so she could at least kiss the walls. She also loved to make genuflections as a devotional practice. When she wanted to make some, she would slyly say to one of the other girls, "Let's measure to see which one of us is taller." While doing the measuring, she could quickly get on and off her knees.

This may have been precocious piety, but not overly so. Elizabeth was still an exuberant child. At the same time, even though she was raised in wealth and luxury, she also became aware of her duties toward her neighbor. When she won something in a game, she would share it with children who were poor.

Elizabeth was educated with great care. The Thuringian dynasty could boast of several learned women. Ludwig III was known to have taken great care over the education of his children; his daughter was renowned for her Latin learning. Even before she learned to read, Elizabeth delighted in poring over the illuminated pictures in the magnificent psalter of the Landgraf's family and would pretend to read from it. The Bible tales and images of Christ and his Mother it contained were her first introduction to the story of salvation. Later, she would learn Latin, as children commonly did, from reading the psalter. We don't know how far she went in her studies, but we do know from later sayings of hers which her handmaids recalled that she also had an excellent memory, and was able to recall many passages from Scripture and sermons she had heard.

But this was only a part of what she had to learn. She also had to know how to sit a horse well, hawk and hunt, and do the finest sewing and needlework. She had to learn court etiquette, and how to direct the servants in their duties. And like all ladies of castles, she learned how to use the power of herbs for healing and studied other traditional medical lore.

Ludwig was probably not educated much with her, for after the age of seven the boys in the family spent most of their time outdoors as they began the physical training that would prepare them for knighthood. Ludwig learned swimming, riding and archery; he trained with the sword and lance in jousting and tournaments. He would have spent some time learning French, the courtly language, and gaining knowledge of the details of political alliances from his father and the other men in the family, which meant spending a great deal of time in their company.

In the evening, though, after dinner, as soon as she was old enough, Elizabeth could go with Ludwig and the other children to the *Sangersaal* to listen to the songs of the Minnesingers and the discussions of chivalry. Hermann I was a great patron of the arts and his court was the center of German literary culture at the time. Wolfram von Eschenbach, the author of the Grail romance *Parzival*, and other poets were often guests.

The subject of all the poems and romances, in one way or another, was love, or *Minne*, who was often personalized as an august goddess-like figure, whether in the form of the heavenly or the earthly Venus. There were poems for every mood. In some, the love of a knight for a lady was noble and exalted. At times, however, the poet hinted that all this suffering for love was a little ridiculous in the sober light of reason. At still other times, as in the Grail romances, courtly love gave way to a higher love. Around the time Elizabeth was born, the poet Hartmann von Aue had sung: "He is truly in love who goes for Love's sake into exile." He was speaking of his journey to confront Saladin's army on the Crusade, a sign of his love for God.[1]

Not all the entertainment was so elevated. Another frequent literary guest at the Wartburg, Walther von der Vogelweide, described in a satirical poem the turbulent life of the castle, where the generous Hermann supplied the visiting boisterous knights with wine, and toasted them from morning till night. He would never let the wine run dry, "even if it cost a thousand pounds a barrel." And then there was the noise! Those who didn't want to grow deaf should avoid the Wartburg.

> I myself have suffered the riffraff's din too long,
> Saw nights grow into days midst shrill,
>   deafening song,
> That people can still hear there, I'll verily deny.[2]

Walther had sensitive ears; Elizabeth on the other hand, had a sensitive nose, as her lady-in-waiting Isentrude recalled. She could not stand bad smells or close air. Inside the rather narrow castle rooms, the mixture of damp air, smoke from the fireplace and the odor of the bodies of knights crowded close together must have been hard for her to bear. She was no doubt very glad that the *kemenate* could be opened to the air by a door on the south, where there was a beautiful arcade, with graceful columns and rounded arches, matching the one that ran around the side of the castle. It must have been lovely to stand there and contemplate the town and distant mountains rising out of the mist.

We learn very little from the sources about the relationship of the future spouses Elizabeth and Ludwig during their early years, but one detail is very telling: they always called each other "brother" and "sister" from their childhood on, even during their married life. When they were younger, of course, that was the type of relationship they experienced; it was more real to them than the distant prospect of being man and wife. But that relationship and the secrets and affection they shared then became the basis for their later love as adults.

Elizabeth's growing love for God led her to want to sacrifice for him. She would leave the game or dance after one round and "give the rest to God." She stopped wearing some of her finery as a sacrifice. Even at this early age she began the process of conversion and penance that is at the heart of Christianity and the Franciscan vocation.

Several early sorrows helped her in this process of renunciation. The first was the death of her mother Gertrude in September 1213, when Elizabeth was six years old. The shocking details of how she met her end may have been kept from the little girl for a time. The truth was that Gertrude had been assassinated.

For some time there had been growing sentiment against the German queen at the Hungarian court, especially after she had given favors and privileges to her own German family that the Hungarian nobles felt should have gone to them. In particular, she arranged to have her brother Berthold, a cleric who was of far from irreproachable character, made the Archbishop of Kalocsa. The nobles became more and more angry at Berthold's arrogance and the queen's extravagance. Andrew was also becoming more and more unpopular because of his reckless spending. When the king and queen were together at the monastery of Lelesz in northern Hungary, Gertrude was attacked and killed. The assassins probably intended to kill Andrew too, but he escaped.

Elizabeth had not seen her mother in more than two years. Now she would not see her again on earth. She must have been deeply affected. When she grew older and had gained more understanding, she would have prayed with particular fervor for her mother's soul, for she had died without the sacraments. In fact, a story preserved by the Anonymous Franciscan says that some years later, Gertrude appeared to Elizabeth in a dream, and asked her daughter to pray that she might be released from purgatory. Elizabeth prayed in earnest, and her mother appeared again to thank her, for her soul had been freed from its pains.[3]

This was only the first of the sorrows Elizabeth had to endure. Hermann, Ludwig's younger brother and Elizabeth's playmate, died in 1216. This was followed by the death of her substitute father, the blustering, hearty Landgraf Herman I on April 25, 1217, when she was ten years old.

His son Ludwig, just seventeen, became the new Landgraf of Thuringia. Here he begins to come into his own, and we can see him as the chroniclers describe him: as an adult. He was of medium height, athletic and handsome. His gracious expression and perfect manners attracted everyone to him. He was measured and sober in speech, and courteous to all women. He was known for his bravery and feats of arms. Once when he came face to face with a lion that had escaped from its cage, he threatened it with his fist, and it lay down submissively.

He was still like an older brother to her, this young man that Elizabeth had always loved and admired, but she understood more now: he was the man who would be her future husband, the one to whom she would be bound in absolute fidelity. The Minnesingers spoke of love as something exalted, yet often the infatuation of love they described was based on air. Elizabeth knew already that the love that would bind her and Ludwig in marriage would be exalted, but it also had to be based on God's will.

Some of her feelings are hinted at in the texts, for instance the candle game. This, Guda tells us, was a game the older girls played. They would write the names of each of the apostles on a candle or a piece of paper, and these would be mixed together and placed on the altar in the chapel. Each girl would draw one to be her special saint. Elizabeth longed to draw the name of the apostle John, who was traditionally thought of as the youngest of the apostles and a virgin; she especially admired him because he was regarded as the guardian of chastity. She prayed hard to win him as her saint and to everyone's amazement, she received his name no less than three times in separate drawings. Was it only her own chastity that Elizabeth was thinking of? Or did she want to ask St. John to guard the chastity of her betrothed? This last seems more likely, because there were so many women saints, including the Blessed Virgin, to guard female chastity, while St. John seems more appropriate for a man.

She would have known that Ludwig was now of an age when his chastity was often under attack. And it would be several years before he and Elizabeth could marry. But he had remained perfectly faithful to his intended bride. So much so that many of the young knights in Ludwig's entourage even questioned his virility and set out to test it.

18

The chaplain Berthold tells us that once, when the Landgraf's family was staying at Ebersburg castle, one of these young blades found a pretty young peasant girl and decided to bring her to Ludwig. He prevailed on her poor family with promises of money and gifts. Elizabeth, playing with the other girls in the castle courtyard, saw the two go inside and understood what was happening; she began to weep and said, "they want to take the precious soul of my brother and condemn it."

The youth knocked on the door of Ludwig's room while he was taking an afternoon nap; he got up and opened the door to see his friend with a girl. When he learned what she was there for, Ludwig spoke to the girl courteously, giving her three silver marks for herself and her family; but he rounded on his young tempter with the strongest possible words. "Escort this young girl home, and if anything happens to her on the way, I will have you hanged." When she saw the young girl leave after such a short time, Elizabeth laughed happily.[4]

As she grew older, Elizabeth began to set stricter standards for herself in regard to the "vanities of the world." She would not sew on her sleeves on Sundays. At this period, sleeves were made separately from the garment, and different sleeves could be sewn into a gown. Women also often laced or sewed their sleeves tightly to fit the outline of the arm, a practice which many preachers condemned as immodest. She also removed her jewels before Mass, which often aroused comment, not all of it complimentary, for while everyone in this society was at least nominally Christian, there were many who liked to be reminded of that fact as little as possible. Some people thought Elizabeth peculiar and whispered about it.

Once on the feast of the Assumption, Elizabeth went with the Landgrafin Sophia and her future sister-in-law Agnes to attend Mass at the Church of Our Lady in Eisenach. They were dressed for the occasion in their most magnificent gowns and crowned with gold and jewels. After a time, however, Elizabeth took off her crown and set it down beside her. This attracted notice all over the church. When Sophia asked her sharply what she was doing, Elizabeth said, "In the presence of God and of my King, Jesus Christ, how can I, a vile and despicable creature, appear before him crowned with the insignia of royal dignity?"[5]

Incidents like this one, which was recounted by Dietrich of Apolda, have often been exaggerated by later writers to suggest that Sophia, and to some extent Agnes, persecuted Elizabeth and made her youth miserable. Sophia, who had taken the place of Elizabeth's mother, naturally had to discipline her according to her understanding of what was proper for a princess. But Sophia was also very devout. There is no reason to believe she was a wicked stepmother type. But her understanding of what she owed to God was always a little different from Elizabeth's. Sophia was always conscious of the dignity of her rank and proper behavior. Elizabeth did not care at all for royal dignity when it came to what she owed God. She would prove this again and again in later years.

III. Marriage and Children

As the time for their marriage approached, events hinted at a possible separation for Elizabeth and Ludwig. Ever since 1215, the emperor Frederick had promised the Pope to go on crusade. When he went, Ludwig, as his vassal, would be asked to go with him.

Throughout the Middle Ages, Jerusalem, the place where Christ suffered, died and rose again, was regarded as a true Christian's spiritual home on earth. The earthly Jerusalem, however, was only the symbol of our true homeland, the heavenly Jerusalem, as described in the Book of Revelation. In earlier centuries, few European Christians could go on a pilgrimage to Jerusalem; it would involve a long trip at a time when travel, especially by sea, was much more dangerous than it is now. But during the Crusades, more and more people "took the cross," which they wore as an emblem, and went to Jerusalem not just as warriors but as pilgrims. Jerusalem, which had been seized from the Muslims in 1099, became the capital of the Christian kingdom of Jerusalem. The later loss of the city to Saladin's army in 1187 reverberated throughout the Christian world.

Pope Innocent III sent out a new crusade call in 1214. Preachers spread the word throughout Germany and aroused tremendous fervor. Everyone spoke about how, on the Friday before Pentecost of that year, in the diocese of Münster, during the crusade preaching, two white crosses appeared in the air facing north and south, and a third in the middle with the figure of the Crucified.[1] There were similar visions and similar excitement all over Germany. Elizabeth's own father, King Andrew of Hungary, left for the East to take part in the assault on Damietta in Egypt.

All this was in everyone's mind when the new Landgraf Ludwig IV was knighted on July 6, 1218 in Eisenach, perhaps in the church of St. George, the patron saint of knights. Elizabeth must have been filled with pride on that day, and thought him the noblest and bravest of men. He was now a Christian knight with the same dignity as his father and grandfather, who had also gone on crusade.

Ludwig wasted no time in showing a boldness fitting to his new rank. He and Siegfried II, the Archbishop of Mainz, were in dispute over the ownership of some land. This seems shocking to us today, but in those days, in addition to being religious leaders, bishops were also feudal lords, and fought to protect their territories as other lords did. Faithful Christians like Ludwig did not feel that opposing a bishop over a temporal matter was wrong. The bishop excommunicated Ludwig, reminding him that his father had also died under a cloud of excommunication, perhaps for a similar reason. Ludwig responded by invading the bishop's lands. The bishop relented and removed the excommunication against both Ludwig and his father. Ludwig was politically ambitious, but unlike his father, he kept his wars away from his own territories so that his own people would not have to suffer.

Elizabeth would always await his return anxiously, her heart beating faster when she saw his horse approaching the castle drawbridge. Her love was now maturing as she did. The most wonderful thing was that Ludwig felt the same way. She would run out to meet him, and he would embrace her and show her the gift he had brought her. Elizabeth was only fourteen, but by the standards of her time, when life spans were shorter, she was already considered an adult and ready to wed.

As the time grew closer for the marriage, however, trouble began to brew. The *Libellus* explains that Ludwig's neighbors, counselors and vassals urged him to repudiate Elizabeth. "They claimed that since with a fatter dowry and the help of his neighbors he could foresee becoming powerful, he should pursue other marriages." In fact, the increase in Elizabeth's dowry, which Queen Gertrude had promised, had not been forthcoming; all her funds had been taken by her brother Berthold when he fled the kingdom on her death. And King Andrew was now a poor man. He had been forced to borrow heavily to finance his own crusade.

Some of Ludwig's supporters advised him to send Elizabeth back to her father. Many criticized her to her face for standing in the way of his advancement. The family also took sides. The Landgrafin Sophia suggested to Elizabeth that she might solve the problem by entering a convent. It was no doubt kindly meant, for Sophia knew of Elizabeth's piety and also shared it. If she couldn't marry Ludwig because of circumstances, she could still be happy serving God as a nun. What did Elizabeth reply? We don't know, but her heart, full of terror and dismay, must have had a number of replies ready: How could what both families had always insisted was right suddenly be wrong? Their betrothal was sanctioned by God! And above all, her heart told her she and Ludwig belonged together.

Ludwig always reassured Elizabeth tenderly in private. But in public he said nothing. Perhaps this in itself was a strategy, or perhaps he didn't take the opposition that seriously. Elizabeth became more and more worried. Walther of Vargila, the knight who had received her from her father, and who had always looked out for her, saw her suffering and took it on himself to find out the truth for her, or perhaps she asked for his help.

When Ludwig and his men were on a hunting trip, Walther found a way to speak to him privately. He asked bluntly: "What do you propose to do with the king's daughter? Are you still going to take her as your wife, or will you send her back to her homeland?"

Perhaps only then did Ludwig understand the seriousness of the situation. He pointed to a high mountain in the distance.

"Truly, if this mountain, which you see, were gold from top to bottom, I would sooner give it up than Elizabeth. Let others think and speak as foolishly as they like; I love Elizabeth, and there is nothing I prefer to marrying her."

Then the knight said, "I ask you my lord, to give me permission to tell her this."

Ludwig said gently, "Tell her, and for a sign that I shall transmit to her, I give her this"; and reaching into his pouch, he gave Walther a closed, double-sided mirror, with bronze backings, mounted in silver: one part plain glass, the other bearing an image of the Crucified. Elizabeth received it with a joyful smile.[2]

Elizabeth's opponents at court, even the Landgraf's family, could not prevail after Ludwig had firmly made his feelings known. And so the wedding was set for sometime in the spring or summer of 1221. Unfortunately even Ludwig's chaplain Berthold failed to record the exact date. We do know that the first official document from Ludwig's reign in which Elizabeth appears as his wife dates from September 9 of that year.[3]

They were wed, as tradition has it, in St. George's church in Eisenach, to the great rejoicing of their people. Elizabeth was fourteen and Ludwig twenty-one. They were a young, attractive glamorous couple. Ludwig was admired for his vigor as a leader, his love of justice and his generosity. Elizabeth's religious devotion and her kindness to the poorest of her people were already well known.

No early description of Elizabeth exists to tell us exactly what she looked like, though garments of hers that have been preserved indicate that she was small in stature. Later writers attributed to her an olive complexion, dark hair and dark eyes. Many who met her during her life found her beautiful, with a radiance due as much to her personality as to her features. On this day, filled as she was with the happiness of a bride, she must have been beautiful indeed.

Around the time of their marriage, the Landgrafin Sophia retired to St. Katherine's Cistercian monastery in Eisenach, which she herself had founded. She had written to Pope Honorius III asking to live under a mitigated form of the Cistercian rule, and to maintain her property so that she could compensate those people her husband had unjustly deprived of their goods in his wars.

Ludwig and Elizabeth were now lord and lady of the Wartburg. It was their official residence and a magnificent one, but they had a number of other castles scattered throughout their territory as well, including the Runneburg and the Neuenburg. They especially loved the sprawling Creuzburg castle a short distance from the Wartburg on the Werra river. Ludwig built a bridge with magnificent Romanesque arches over the river for easier access to the castle and to improve the trade route there.

On September 29, 1221, Ludwig and Elizabeth set out with a large retinue to visit her father in Hungary, a journey that would take weeks. The trip was no doubt a wedding present from Ludwig to Elizabeth, who must have wanted nothing so much as to visit the father she had not seen since she was four years old. Ludwig himself may have wanted to raise the question of the promised addition to Elizabeth's dowry, but when they arrived, he could see that there was little hope of this.

Andrew, whose crusade had failed, and whose riches were gone, had been forced by his nobles to grant them a number of privileges that stripped him of some of his power. There was even talk of putting his son, sixteen-year-old son Béla, on the throne instead. Andrew was now a sad and broken man, but throughout his life he had a particular concern for this daughter who lived so far from him. And now she had happy news to tell him: she would soon bear him a grandchild.

When the young couple returned to Thuringia, they seemed to have had a short time when Ludwig did not have to travel, and they could remain together, making plans for the coming child. But Ludwig was soon on the road again, seeing to the business of his territories. Elizabeth retired to Creuzburg castle, less hectic than the Wartburg, for the birth of her child. Ludwig was in Marburg in Hesse, on the edge of his territories, meeting with the burghers of the city in the main church of the town, when a messenger arrived: It was the best possible news: the birth of a son and heir on March 28 1222; the boy was named Hermann after his grandfather.

Elizabeth understood that marriage was not just a means to happiness or personal fulfillment, but a vocation, as serious as the religious vocation, and a means by which she was called to achieve holiness. Our love of those close to us is the root of our understanding of love in general, and most of all, of how we are to love God. This is true of married love, for, as the Second Vatican Council tells us, this love "wells up from the fountain of divine love," that is, it has its origin in God; the Council adds that "authentic married love is caught up into divine love."[4]

Little attention has been paid to marriage when discussing the lives of the saints. In fact, Elizabeth is one of the very few married people canonized until just recently. Her husband is also popularly regarded as a saint. But marriage as a source of holiness or a vocation has often been downplayed in lives of married saints by clerical writers. But Elizabeth and the immediate witnesses to her life saw things differently. According to the *Libellus*, Elizabeth herself explained why she dressed well for her husband: "Because I want him to love me alone with proper marital affection, so that from Him who has sanctified the law of marriage, we may await together the reward of eternal life." Isentrude, who knew more about Elizabeth than anyone, said that she and her husband "lived in marriage in a way worthy of praise. They loved each other with a wonderful affection, gently encouraging and strengthening each other in the praise and service of God."

It is important to remember that Elizabeth and Ludwig were saints not because they had no problems, but because they overcame their problems. One was that they lived in a very immoral atmosphere at court, amid many temptations, which the writers of the time don't try to hide from us. But they were resolute in avoiding these traps. Ludwig's men actually expressed to him their surprise that he was not unfaithful to his wife. He replied, "Never mention these words to me again: I have a wife, with whom I am bound to keep faith."[5] Elizabeth also had to deal with some long separations from her husband, who traveled very frequently dealing with the affairs of his territories. When he was away, she withdrew from court parties and entertainments and spent her time in prayer, to withdraw from any worldly distractions and temptations.

Frequently she would get up at night to pray, while Ludwig, concerned about her discomfort, would hold her hands, begging her to get back in bed. Perhaps because of his concern, Elizabeth then began to ask her ladies-in-waiting to wake her at night for prayer while her husband was sleeping (or pretending to), by pulling her foot. Once Isentrude, in trying to wake her, pulled Ludwig's foot by mistake, for he had extended his leg over to his wife's side of the bed. He woke up, but "knowing her intention, bore it patiently."

Because of the length of her prayers, Elizabeth often fell asleep on the carpet in front of the bed. When her handmaids found fault with her for this, and asked why she did not sleep in bed beside her husband, she answered: "Although I cannot always pray, I can do violence to my flesh by tearing myself away from my beloved husband." Elizabeth spoke with the feelings of someone whom marriage had truly made "one flesh" with her spouse.

Ludwig was often away on military adventures. One was the result of an ugly family quarrel. In 1221, Dietrich, the Markgrafin of Meissen, husband of Ludwig's older half-sister, Jutta, died. Before his death, he had asked Ludwig to be the guardian of their young son Heinrich and regent of the territories he would govern. But Jutta came to resent what she felt to be Ludwig's interference in her lands, and to counter this, secretly planned to marry a powerful lord named Poppo of Henneburg to take over from her brother.

When Ludwig found out about this violation of his rights, he was furious, and at the beginning of 1223, the two ended up going to war. Ludwig defeated his sister's troops, and in order to ensure her compliance in his terms, took his young nephew Heinrich hostage. Peace was made by Elizabeth's maternal uncle, Otho of Meran. Perhaps Elizabeth herself, distressed at the quarrel, encouraged him in his peacemaking.

Then, in 1223, Ludwig received his Crusade call from Pope Honorius III. The emperor Frederick offered him 4,000 marks to cover his expenses. The Pope offered to put his lands under the protection of the Church. Everyone wondered what he would do; some even criticized him for delaying. He had so much to live for!

In may have been about this time that Walther von der Vogelweide, who had known his father so well, wrote a poem as a warning to Ludwig about neglect of duty; the duty is unspecified, but most commentators believe he meant Ludwig's seeming reluctance to take the cross:

> Whoever, for his courtly breeding and civility,
> Sits in the noble Landgrave's council,
>> ministerial or free,
> Remind him kindly of my counsels,
> so there's some effect on him I see.
> My youthful lord is known as generous,
>> they tell me he is steadfast,
> Well bred also; celebrated qualities, all three.
> If he fulfilled the fourth good quality in earnest,
> He would be walking straight –
>> his step unfailing, unembarrassed.
> Free of negligence. Neglect undoes the sowing,
>> kills the harvest.[6]

In May of 1224, Ludwig attended the imperial Diet (a meeting of German princes with the emperor) in Frankfort, and the question of the crusade was discussed. This time Frederick offered Ludwig 5,000 marks and agreed to pay his travel expenses. After deliberation, Ludwig announced that he would take the cross. The glad news went out among all the clergy of Germany, who knew that the pious decision of such an important ruler would encourage the other nobles to do the same. It was something that Elizabeth had feared, but she consoled herself with the knowledge that his departure would be delayed for a time, perhaps a year or more.

Elizabeth's second child, a daughter, Sophia, was born on March 24, 1224, two years almost to the day after her brother's birth. As she did at the births of each of her children, Elizabeth went to church forty days afterward to take part in the rite of purification, in which she imitated Mary's journey to Jerusalem for the rite of purification after Jesus' birth. Medieval liturgists explained that the journey to the earthly church or temple which the rite involved was also a foretaste of our whole life's journey to the temple of the heavenly Jerusalem, and the period of forty days after childbirth represented our earthly life. This understanding of the rite as a spiritual journey to Jerusalem must have been greatly heightened in Elizabeth's time by the enthusiasm for the crusades and for visiting the Holy Land, and most of all for the hoped-for recapture of Jerusalem.

Elizabeth took the rite very seriously. While other noblewomen appeared with a large retinue, grandly dressed, she came in private with her child in her arms, dressed in wool and barefoot. The author of the *Libellus*, who had visited Elizabeth's home as a pilgrim, describes her as making the long trek from a rocky road leading from the castle to the church in Eisenach.

The rite would have begun during the procession to the church, with the praying of Psalm 120, one of the "songs of ascent" of Jewish pilgrims as they too went to Jerusalem along a rocky path, and lifted their eyes to the hills surrounding the city, praying for protection on their journey: "I lift up my eyes to the mountains: from where shall help come to me? My help shall come from the Lord who made heaven and earth." When Elizabeth approached the door of the church, the priest prayed: "Lord, Our God, bless this your servant, presented to You after childbirth at your temple to be purified by grace; and kindly grant, that just as we are introducing her by our office into this earthly temple, after the end of this life of penance, she may deserve to enter heaven." As Elizabeth was led into the church, the priest prayed: "Enter into the temple of God so that you may have eternal life. Amen."[7]

Inside the church, a second ceremony took place, the dedication of her child, modeled after the presentation of the

Child Jesus in the temple. Elizabeth offered her child, a lamb, and a candle at the altar. After the ceremony, she would give the penitential garment she had worn to a poor woman.

As the wife of a future crusader, the idea of a pilgrimage to Jerusalem represented in this rite would have had a special meaning for Elizabeth. She was not going to be able to make the journey with Ludwig, but now she was making it in spirit. It was also a foretaste of her later life of penance as a Franciscan.

The young Landgrafin took full part in the life of her people in the town of Eisenach and the surrounding villages. She would join in the procession on Rogation Days, which were held on April 25 and the three days preceding Ascension Thursday, to ask God's blessing on the crops. As the priest and people walked through the fields, they sang the Litany of the Saints, and there would be stations, or stops, at churches along the way. Elizabeth would always walk in procession among the poorest women and stand with them at the stations to listen to the sermon.

On Holy Thursday she would wash the feet of the lepers and speak to them in her gentle voice of faith and patience.

Dietrich of Apolda describes how, when she awoke on Good Friday, she would say to her ladies-in-waiting: "Today is the day of humiliation, I don't want you to show me any reverence." She would dress in the clothes of a peasant and mingle with the poor of Eisenach as they went to the altars of each church in town. There she would leave the customary gifts of flax, incense and candles on the altar. Then she would go outside in the crowd and give the coins in her apron to poor beggars.[8]

These contacts made Elizabeth more and more aware of the suffering of the poor, and helping them came to take up more and more of her time. When one of the local peasants had a child, Elizabeth would stand as godmother. The poor came to trust her so much that they would send for her in any need and she would come to help them. She entered their poor hovels, and did everything she could for those who were in financial straits or ill or suffering. She even offered to milk a cow for a sick person who was thirsty —or tried to, for the cow would not even allow her to get close.

Elizabeth also did everything she could to preserve the dignity of the poor people she came in contact with. Knowing that the poor often did not have shrouds, she would provide shrouds of the best linen and prepare them for burial with her own hands. She could not stand to see the rich buried in fine garments, feeling that these should be used to bury the poor. At that time, the lives of mothers-to-be and their children were often threatened by poverty as they are today. Elizabeth provided for pregnant women, making sure that they had enough food, money and clothing to care for themselves and their newborns.

In his Testament, St. Francis said that the true beginning of his conversion was his encounter with the lepers. He saw the suffering of Christ in them. Elizabeth too saw Christ in the lepers and all of the poor. Dietrich of Apolda recounts how Elizabeth once placed a leper in the bed she shared with her husband. Her mother-in-law, Sophia, was horrified, and called on her son to stop this kind of charity. But when Ludwig looked at the bed, he saw in his heart Christ on the crucifix there.[9]

Elizabeth lived as a rich woman in a castle, but could not ignore what went on in the outside world. She became aware of the human misery that surrounded her. She went out to encounter and help the poor, and they in turn, changed her. She came to care less and less for court life, and grew restless with the desire to grow closer to God.

IV. The Minstrels of God

Elizabeth received a gift that corresponded to her desire when she first met the Franciscan friars, who had only recently made their way into Germany. We don't know the exact date the meeting took place, but it was a major turning point in her life.

At the chapter of 1217, Francis, in his fervor for preaching penance, had sent a group of friars to Germany, where they were at first given hospitality. But later their practice of poverty led people to regard them as a group like the Patarines, heretics who lived in Lombardy, or the Cathars, many of whom were found in the Rhineland, and they ended up driving them from the country. Francis was undaunted. In 1221 he sent a second delegation, headed by Brother Caesarius of Speyer. Many of them must have thought they were going to their deaths. Brother Giordano of Giano certainly did. He had never even intended to volunteer. He just went among the others and spoke to them, pleased to have contact with those who were so brave, until one of them playfully forced him to sit among them, and his name too was put down. He later became the chronicler of the mission, which was to succeed beyond their wildest dreams.

When they reached Augsburg, the bishop welcomed them, and the city became their headquarters. They divided into three groups: one that headed towards Salzburg, another to Regensburg, and the third north and west to Würzburg, Mainz,

Worms, Speyer, and Cologne. This last group was headed by John of Pian Carpino; among them was a lay brother named Rudeger, whom the friars had received into the order in Würzburg on their way north. Towards the end of 1223 they arrived in Hildesheim in Lower Saxony, and asked the bishop, Conrad, for permission to preach, which he granted. They soon had foundations in Goslar and Halberstadt. From there they crossed over into Thuringia. It was probably sometime in 1224 that Rudeger and his companions came to the Wartburg and Elizabeth first learned of the romance of St. Francis and his Lady Poverty from the "minstrels of God."

Of all the songs of courtly love and chivalrous romances that Elizabeth had listened to in her life, this was the most wonderful, the one that most touched her heart.[1] They told how Francis had renounced his wealth and given everything to the poor, how he attracted followers, how Pope Innocent III himself had been moved by the purity of their following of the Gospel and approved their rule, and how Francis and his friars went barefoot and begging throughout the world. Their words echoed everything Elizabeth was already feeling, her dissatisfaction with riches and her love for the poor. And she was not one to love without acting. She saw to it that the friars were fed and clothed so they could carry on their work. She even spun the wool for their habits herself. Not only that, she began to long to live as they did, and to experience the peace so evident in their lives. Isentrude later recalled how Elizabeth would dress in a shabby cloak in front of her ladies and wrap a cheap, coarse piece of cloth around her head, telling them, "This is how I will walk when I go begging and bear misery for the love of God." At that time, she was no more than seventeen or eighteen years old.

Brother Rudeger, as Giordano tells us, became "Blessed Elizabeth's master of spiritual discipline, teaching her to preserve chastity, humility and patience, to keep watch in prayer and to apply herself to works of mercy."[2] Though Rudeger was able to give Elizabeth spiritual advice, he was a not a priest and could not have acted as her confessor.

At the end of 1224, Giordano of Giano, now *custos*, or regional superior, for Thuringia, arrived in Erfurt, the major city in the territory, with his friars, where they lodged in a chapel belonging to a leper hospital outside the city walls. In 1225, Giordano sent friars to canvas all the towns in the territory with the object of founding houses there. When a friar named Hermann came to Eisenach to preach, he was so successful that several churches were offered to him, and Giordano chose the place for the foundation. It is not clear if Elizabeth had a part in establishing this friary, or whether this was the first Franciscan foundation in Eisenach, for Elizabeth may have given the friars a small chapel earlier, the one mentioned by Conrad in his letter.[3]

There is evidence as well that Elizabeth had a house built for the friars as early as 1225 on the lands granted to her by her husband as her dower in Marburg in Hesse.[4] Like the other earliest Franciscan foundations, it was on the outskirts of town, on the banks of the Lahn river. They probably received an already-existing church or chapel; Elizabeth had a small house built for them. The Anonymous Franciscan is the only thirteenth-century source to give us any details about this little foundation; he describes it as "the place where the friars were received" or the "house of the friars" rather than as a convent, so it must have been a small, poor place, in accordance with the will of St. Francis.

Here we come to the much-discussed question of whether it was at this time that Elizabeth became a member of the "Brothers and Sisters of Penance," or Third Order, the forerunner of today's Secular Franciscans. It is very difficult to give a definite answer. Records about Franciscan penitents in Germany are nonexistent for this period. We know of two letters of St.

Francis to the penitents and of the rule, called the *Memoriale Propositi,* used as early as 1221 by Italian penitents living in their own homes, a rule which was similar to that of many other penitential groups. But is there any evidence that the friars could have brought knowledge of this way of life with them to the Wartburg this early?

The heart of the Franciscan ideal of the penitential life can be found in Francis' letters to the Brothers and Sisters of Penance, in which he urges them to love God with their whole hearts and their neighbors as themselves, to turn completely away from sin, and to bring forth "fruits worthy of penance" in active works of love for God and others. Entrance into the penitential state was marked by a change in dress, and a solemn vow to commit to this way of life.

In his letters, St. Francis also insisted that penitents restore goods acquired by fraud and usury.[5] This was regarded not only as an unlawful means of profit, and something that took the soul away from God, but as something that hurt the needy borrower and broke solidarity with the poor. Many of the Franciscan penitents in urban and commercial Italy, where usury was common, gave great importance to this precept, including Blessed Umiliana dei Cerchi in Florence, who urged her husband to return the usurious interest he was keeping. This concern was also shared by other penitential groups.

The early Franciscan penitents in Italy were also strongly influenced by the idea of the political *comune* of the Italian city states, which brought nobles and artisans, rich and poor together in the experience of political community. The Italian penitential fraternities brought the same diverse groups in society together in their common spiritual ties. The aim was to achieve a stronger sense of brotherhood among all classes.

It is possible that Rudeger and the other friars who advised Elizabeth knew about the penitential fraternities in Italy and were acquainted with the *Memoriale Propositi*. In fact, many aspects of the way of life that Elizabeth adopted during her marriage do appear to be consonant with this rule and Francis' exhortations to penitents. These included her wearing of a simple penitential style of dress, and her avoidance of silk ribbons and other adornments, as well as dances and other entertainments; not to mention her active charity and strong sense of justice in regard to defrauding the poor, as we will see later.

Elizabeth may have adopted many of the practices of a penitential rule such as the *Memoriale Propositi* in an informal way during her married life. But this is the most we can say. None of the witnesses describe her making a profession as a penitent or following a rule during her marriage. The only profession any of them mentions took place after her husband's death. Nevertheless, her way of life is the model for the one that Secular Franciscans live today, and she is rightly celebrated as our patron saint.

Elizabeth was greatly devoted not only to the friars but to the poor man Francis himself, according to what the Anonymous Franciscan tells us. He says that once when Cardinal Ugolino, the protector of the friars and the future Pope Gregory IX, was visiting with Francis, he told the saint about the great things he had heard about Elizabeth's humility and love of poverty, and taking the mantle from Francis shoulders, suggested that he send it "to his most humble German daughter" as a tribute to her holiness. The author adds that Elizabeth put on this mantle every time she wanted to ask something special of God.[6]

When we look at these years, we get the impression that Elizabeth grew steadily in holiness. Yet there are some signs in the sources that she also experienced a spiritual dryness, a tribulation that affects many souls just as they seem to be approaching true union with God. There could have been many causes. We can only guess at them.

More and more, as she obtained a clearer vision of God and true awe in his presence, perhaps she came to feel her littleness and sinfulness even more. Perhaps, as she came to desire to spend more and more time in prayer, she was frustrated by the many tasks of her daily life. Perhaps she was beginning to feel guilty because she and her husband lived in such magnificence while the peasants who worked for them had nothing. She took care of their needs as best she could, but was that enough?

It also seems that she may have felt unworthy because she could not live the perfect life of a consecrated virgin. The clerical ideas of the time did not look favorably on marriage as a help to life with God. The cloister was regarded as the ideal to which every soul longing for perfection should strive. And that chance had passed Elizabeth by when she had chosen to marry Ludwig. Whatever the cause, God, who had always been so close, suddenly seemed very far away.

Something of this is suggested in a story which may go back to an early witness, the chaplain Berthold, and is recorded in the *Chronicle of Reinhardsbrunn*. One day, the Landgraf Ludwig was bled—something which was regarded as a healthy purgative at the time. Since he was kept indoors that day, he gave a banquet for his friends. All the guests were in the chapel, dressed in their best for Mass. During the consecration, Elizabeth found herself looking with love at her husband instead of at the altar. But Christ immediately reproached her: when she glanced back at the altar, she saw in the priest's hands not a host, but the crucified Christ dripping with blood. Filled with guilt, she prostrated herself weeping on the ground; she would not go in to dinner. When Ludwig came to see what had happened, he saw her eyes red with weeping. Unable to persuade her to tell him what was wrong, he went away with tears in his own eyes.[7]

Whether the story is true literally or only symbolically, it gives us an idea of the conflict Elizabeth may have experienced in her soul. Psychologically, it is also very perceptive. Until now, Elizabeth had shared everything with her husband. All that we know about Ludwig indicates that he was devout, but his was more of a soldier's simple piety. He might not have understood her mystical aspirations and her inner turmoil. And how could she have explained the experience that led her to feel that he was a rival to God, who was now demanding everything from her? This was a torment for Elizabeth for which she had no solution.

V. Master Conrad

Toward the end of 1225, the crusade preacher Master Conrad of Marburg arrived at the Wartburg. He was to be another momentous influence in Elizabeth's life, and whether this influence was for good or ill has been greatly debated. We know little about Conrad's background, apart from the fact that he was from Marburg, and as the title "Master" given to him indicates, he was educated at a university, perhaps the University of Paris. If so, this would tell us a great deal about the type of instruction he gave Elizabeth, for Paris was the center of several moral and spiritual reform movements in the Church at this time, among them the one centered around Peter Cantor.

This reform movement was deeply concerned with the life of penance and love manifested in works of charity. Other reformers, including Jacques de Vitry and Robert Courzon, directed new forms of religious life for women. Conrad also had friends in the new Franciscan and Dominican orders. He must have been well known and trusted in Rome, for preaching the crusade in Germany was a momentous task, given only to the most highly-regarded priests. The area was certainly facing grave spiritual problems.

One of the most serious was the widespread influence of heretical groups such as the Cathars and the Poor of Lyons. Much of their appeal was due to their claim to be living the true

Christian life because of their austerity, which contrasted with the luxurious living of many clerics. The Pope was anxious to have a man of true Christian zeal represent the Church in the task of preaching reform and recruiting for the crusade.

In Conrad's case, rigorous intellect and burning zeal were combined with the strictest austerity of life. He was a secular cleric, not a religious, and not vowed to poverty, but he refused all the goods of the world; he did not have a prebend (that is, the right of a member of a cathedral chapter to his share of the revenues), nor any church of his own. He fasted constantly and treated his body harshly. Refusing a horse, he rode around everywhere on a mule, surrounding by crowds of people who eagerly attended his sermons. Many people felt that such rejection of wealth was the sign of a true Christian.

Perhaps Conrad had come to the Wartburg as a result of Ludwig's taking of the cross. He would have looked on it as his duty to direct Ludwig, a relative of the Emperor and an acknowledged leader among the German princes, in the proper fulfilling of his crusading vow, and also to guide his wife Elizabeth in her spiritual preparation for this sacrifice.

At any rate, Conrad's influence at the Thuringian court was enormous. Caesarius of Heisterbach tells us: "The Landgraf Ludwig and his wife, blessed Elizabeth, were ruled in all spiritual matters by his advice."[1] In fact, Elizabeth took Conrad as her confessor, and with her husband's consent, made a vow of obedience to him.

Historians have often wondered why Elizabeth did not make her vow of obedience to a Franciscan. There are several possible reasons. The Franciscan order in Germany at this time had very few priests, not even enough to serve all of the new foundations, as Giordano lamented.[2] They most likely could not spare one to be Elizabeth's confessor. In addition, the First Rule

41

of St. Francis forbade the friars to receive promises of obedience from women.

This prohibition was not repeated in the definitive rule of 1223, but seems to have been very much in its spirit. It was probably adopted as much on account of Francis' reluctance to see the friars in positions of authority as out of fear of the scandal that might be caused by too great a familiarity with women. And Conrad, unlike Rudeger, was a priest and thus was able to be Elizabeth's confessor as well as her spiritual director.

Some years later, when Conrad wrote to the Pope about his first encounters with Elizabeth, he said that he had found her "lamenting that she had ever married, and that she had not been able to end her life in the flower of her virginity." This does not sound like Elizabeth at all, for we know how much she loved her husband, and had desired to marry him. Modern biographers believe that this should be understood as Elizabeth regretting that she could not live what was regarded as the more perfect life—as a virgin dedicated to God. Her doubts may have originated from the conflict she felt between the demands of loving both God and her husband. There is also the possibility that Conrad exaggerated Elizabeth's regrets somewhat in a letter that was intended as part of a campaign for her canonization, for even married saints were expected to have a strong desire for the religious life. It was considered most meritorious and a proof of sanctity if a woman longed to leave married life for the cloister.

Perhaps it was in connection with her doubts that, sometime in late 1225 or the beginning of 1226, Elizabeth made another vow with her hands in Master Conrad's: to preserve continence after her husband's death. It was also no doubt part of her preparations for Ludwig's departure for the Crusade; it was a decision about her future life if he were to be killed in battle. Her handmaids, the unmarried Guda, and the widowed Isentrude, made vows of chastity at the same time. This took place in St.

Katherine's Cistercian monastery in Eisenach, where her mother-in-law Sophia had retired in 1221; she was most likely present at the ceremony. Perhaps the fact that the vow was taken here was a sign that the family expected Elizabeth to retire to this same monastery, along with her ladies, on her own husband's death. True, Elizabeth had already experienced an attraction to the Franciscan life of poverty and begging, but she was still a long way from actually making plans to follow it.

Master Conrad held Elizabeth strictly to her conscience in all things. And there was something that had been troubling her conscience ever since she had seen how the peasants in her husband's lands lived: she had seen the heavy exaction of taxes from them and the fraud that went along with it. The ideals of poverty brought to her by the Franciscans and her acquaintance with the penitential movement increased her awareness of this. The penitents in urban Italy were often preoccupied with the injustice of usury, but the injustices committed by feudal lords were just as serious, and it was these that came to Elizabeth's attention.

Isentrude, who gives such exact details, is once again our guide: "After Elizabeth had promised obedience to him, Master Conrad directed her not to make use of any of her husband's goods about which she did not have a clear conscience. She abstained from everything that came from offices and the profits taken by officials, not using foods unless she knew that they came from her husband's own revenues and his legitimate possessions." There are two principles at stake in these words. First, the Landgraf's officials, the *ministeriales*, took taxes in kind (food they had grown, animals, etc) from the peasants throughout his provinces of Thuringia, Saxony and Hesse. But many took much more than they should, so they could take a higher commission for themselves, which amounted to unjust extortion. By restricting herself to the goods taken from her husband's *desmene* (the land directly around the Wartburg), which were gathered by trusted officials from their household, Elizabeth could be sure the goods were taken justly. Another question was whether some of the goods might have been taken from lands belonging to the Church that Ludwig had wrongly claimed as his, or from other properties he had invaded. Any taxes taken from these lands would not be regarded as being from his legitimate possessions, and so would be unlawful, and partaking of them would be unjust.

Three of Elizabeth's ladies-in-waiting joined with her in this fast of conscience, which might even be described as a boycott. Elizabeth undertook it with some trepidation. Would it harm her husband's authority or reputation with his men? She went with her ladies to ask Ludwig whether he would be offended by it. Ludwig himself was well aware of his duties in regard to justice and where his administration was lacking, and he knew that he himself bore responsibility for it. He reassured Elizabeth: "I would gladly do the very same thing, if I did not fear insults from the family and from others. Nevertheless, God willing, I will soon arrange my state of life differently." One of the most admirable things about Ludwig is that he respected Elizabeth's conscience in this delicate case, as he did in all matters, even when it caused him difficulties.

Indeed, fear of causing him difficulties was undoubtedly what led Elizabeth to not make a show of what she was doing. She would sit at table at banquets in front of knights and ladies who looked on curiously, and in the sight of the servants of those officials who perpetrated the fraud, or perhaps the officials themselves. When the extorted food was served, she would cut it up and move it here and there, pretending to eat it; nevertheless people noticed. In order to be certain about what she was eating, she would question the servants of the estate managers, who brought the food to the Landgraf's kitchens, before she would eat any of it. At banquets at court, Ludwig, who sat next to her, was often able to give her exact and reassuring details about the provenance of the foods being served, but Elizabeth still often found herself going hungry at the rich table, in front of the most tempting and delicious-smelling dishes.

As she did with everything, Elizabeth made a game out of it. When she came back from her questioning of the servants, she would tell her ladies, "You are going to eat only," or "You are going to drink only." But when she found out that both were licit, she would clap her hands merrily and say, "Good for us, now we are going to eat and drink."

They ran into difficulties in traveling as well. On her way to join her husband at the Diet in Würzburg in November 1226, Elizabeth discovered that she could not eat from the provender that was carried in the wagons, nor could anything licit be bought on the way. She and her maids lived on black bread softened in water during the whole trip.

Elizabeth suffered for a long time from hunger because of her determination to obey her conscience. But, adds Isentrude, she did establish a network of friends and places legitimate food could be bought, through which she was gradually able to get enough to eat. Most important, she had the income from the property assigned to her by her husband's family as her dower, the property intended to support her in the event of his death.

To understand the question fully, it is important to know that the land and goods of the ruling family of Thuringia were held in common by all the family members. Wives' dowers were included in the family inheritance, and the revenues came out of the joint pool of property. After the death of her husband, however, a widow could choose either to continue to share in the community property and receive her sustenance (*sustentatio*) from it, or to receive any assets which belonged to her, including money, jewels and precious objects, along with the separate income from her dower, which she could administer as she wished, though the land itself did not belong to her.

Isentrude says that Elizabeth provided for her handmaids and herself out of her dower property. In order to do this and avoid any income from tainted revenues, she would have had to administer this property herself as income separate from the joint revenues of the family, even though it was not customary for a wife to do so during her husband's lifetime. We do know that wives of the ruling family received their properties—castles and the fiefs around them—in the outlying territories of their husband's jurisdiction. According to the *Libellus*, Elizabeth's dower was the town and castle of Marburg in Hesse, at the edge of her husband's lands. As administrator, she could choose only honest officials and servants to collect taxes, and could make sure that goods were not extorted from the tenants. We can be sure that Ludwig would have helped her accomplish this, though the transfer of officials might have taken some time. Because of this, Elizabeth had considerable power and administrative authority at her disposal. Ludwig's family however, was impatient with all this.

They would insult him and Elizabeth to their faces. Why did he allow Elizabeth to influence the collection of taxes? Should they not take what was due them? How could the family maintain themselves otherwise? Power and wealth seemed to be more important to them than conscience. Ludwig's younger brothers, Heinrich Raspe and Conrad, had a particular stake in the question, as they would end up ruling in Thuringia if Ludwig died before his son Hermann reached his majority.

More and more Elizabeth began to long for a chance to escape with her husband from this way of life. Ludwig must have known that she wanted to give away everything so that her love of God might be unimpeded, even if she didn't speak of it directly.

He himself later told the following story to Dietrich, the Bishop of Trier, who eventually told it to Elizabeth's biographer, Caesarius of Heisterbach. One night, when they were lying awake together in bed, Elizabeth said to her husband, "I have been thinking about the good life, the life we need, one where we can usefully serve God."

"What is that life?" Ludwig asked.

"I would like us to have only a hundred acres of land or so, and two hundred sheep; you could cultivate the land with your own hands and I would milk the sheep."

Ludwig smiled. "Ah! sister, if we had a hundred acres of land and two hundred sheep, we would not be poor, but rich."[3] But still, he knew what Elizabeth was thinking: that their possessions were harming their souls.

At Conrad's command, Elizabeth sometimes flagellated herself at night when her husband was asleep. She had previously done this on Fridays and during Lent; now she did it more frequently under Conrad's direction. He insisted on strict obedience to his orders. One day Elizabeth was unable to come at his command to one of his sermons because of a visit by her husband's sister Jutta, the Markgrafin of Meissen, with whom Ludwig had recently been in conflict over their territories. Elizabeth's welcome of her sister-in-law was politically important for her husband. But when Conrad heard of it, he told her he would not have charge of her any longer. When she and her ladies, Guda and Isentrude, fell at his feet and begged for forgiveness, he decided on a penance: he had them stripped to their undergarments and flagellated. His attitude to Elizabeth up until her death was marked by this kind of severity.

Conrad's relationship with Elizabeth has always been one of the most controversial elements of her life, and historians have often found her attachment to him hard to explain. In most ways, he was her opposite in character, and there seems to have been little sympathy between their souls. Conrad, it seems, was bent on detaching Elizabeth from all earthly loves, so that she could belong entirely to God. Elizabeth's natural inclination was to love God through her love of husband, children, and her neighbors. Above all, there seems to have been very little joy in Conrad's spirituality, while Elizabeth's love for God naturally flowed into the joy and optimism we so love in her character.

The beatings he gave her are troubling too. Though it is completely alien to the thought of our time, flagellation was a common ascetic and penitential practice in the Middle Ages, and even before she met Conrad, Elizabeth had practiced it on occasion. But Conrad's treatment of her went far beyond the norm considered acceptable at the time. In the Rule of St. Benedict, for instance, flagellation as a punishment was severely regulated and was to be used as a last resort; Conrad was apparently not inhibited by any such considerations. Later, after her husband's death, he would not restrict himself to these beatings, but would slap her in the face if she disobeyed his commands.

And we have to ask: why would Elizabeth have put up with his cruel treatment of her? The question is particularly troubling to us today when we are very aware of the problem of battered wives and other female victims of male violence. Conrad certainly must have been a charismatic man, as the crowds surrounding him wherever he went and the popularity of his preaching attest. It may be that Elizabeth fell under his spell, and the violent side of his personally began to show itself only later (as is often true of batterers). Perhaps at that time she was seeking in him a strong ally in her desire to practice complete poverty, for as much as Ludwig loved her, he could not completely share this ideal, not without renouncing his own power. In fact, much later, Elizabeth was to tell one of her sisters at the hospital, Irmingard, that she had chosen Conrad personally for her confessor and chose him because of his extreme poverty: "I could have promised obedience to some of the bishops or abbots who have possessions, but I thought it best to promise to Master Conrad, who does not have any, but is a complete beggar, so that I might have no consolation in this life."

Elizabeth does seem to have received very little earthly consolation from Conrad. And his heavenly consolation was of a very bleak and wintry kind. She did confide some of her spiritual troubles to him, and he certainly did well to reinforce her conscience when it came to unjust food. But this severe priest was not the type to deal effectively with the spiritual questions troubling Elizabeth most deeply. She fought those out alone, at least for a time.

This was partly because her friends the Franciscans were very busy. They were founding convents in Germany at a tremendous rate; the impression Giordano of Giano leaves us is that they were almost constantly on the road. Consequently, Rudeger and the other friars were not able to visit Elizabeth very often. This is one of the areas of her life where we would most like to know more details. The closest we can get to them is a story reported by a Franciscan source, the *Chronicle of the Twenty- Four Generals of the Order of Minors*, that appears to rely on the memories of the friars who knew her. It describes how her husband saw her wasting away with sadness, and asked her why. She said that she had not seen the friars for a long time, and had been deprived of the spiritual nourishment she had received from them. Ludwig, who was always attentive to her needs, quickly sent for two Franciscans to come and see her. They talked together about God as they walked by the river. Elizabeth said to one of them: "One thing above all pierces my heart, dearest Father: I feel, perhaps because of my sins, that God loves me little, although I try to love him as much as I can; and that is why I fear greatly that he will reject me as unworthy of his love."

The brother, who was particularly gifted with spiritual wisdom, answered that God loved her infinitely more than she loved him. "If this were true," Elizabeth insisted, "He would not permit me to be separated from him, even for a moment, by so many miseries and weaknesses." The friar continued to argue the opposite. Finally, Elizabeth, pointing to a tree on the opposite bank of the river, said, "I would sooner believe that the tree over there can transfer itself to the other side of the river than that God could forget me so in these calamities, if he loves me out of his sweetness as I love him." She had scarcely finished speaking when the tree immediately came out of the ground by its roots and crossed the river. Elizabeth now believed in the brother's words and gave thanks to God.[4]

This is one of the stories about Elizabeth that I would most like to believe true, for it shows her to be so human, seeking for understanding. Her husband would certainly not be thought good if he neglected to let her know that he loved her. Why then did God seemingly withdraw from her? This sense of abandonment is one of the greatest mysteries of our relationship with God. It is the "dark night of the soul" that John of the Cross described a few centuries later. But Elizabeth's contemporary, the mystic Mechtild of Magdeburg, felt it as well, and also described the remedy for it in her words to God: "Since you have taken from me all that I had of you, yet of your grace leave me the gift which every dog has by nature: that of being true to you in my distress, when I am deprived of all consolation. This I desire more fervently than I do your heavenly Kingdom."[5] Elizabeth did not yet understand, though she later would, that when God lets go of our hand, it is because he wants us to learn to walk on our own.

❧

VI. The Mother of the Poor

Early in the spring of 1226, Ludwig departed for Italy, for Frederick II had called an Imperial Diet in Cremona, where he planned to meet with his vassals, including the German princes and representatives of those cities of Lombardy that were loyal to him. They were to discuss the best way to combat heresy and to prepare for the coming crusade. But Milan and some other Lombard cities, traditionally hostile to the Emperor, rose in rebellion; their troops blocked the Brenner Pass in the mountains, which the Germans had to cross to get to Verona and go south. Ludwig and a few others managed to get through the pass and meet the Emperor at his palace in Ravenna.

Ludwig's time there would not have been dull. The Emperor Frederick, known to many then and since as *Stupor Mundi*, "The Amazement of the World," was a man not only of boundless ambition but of a restless mind and passionate curiosity: he welcomed not only poets, but scientists and philosophers to his court and the discussion there were wide-ranging; he also kept a menagerie of wild beasts, including some never before seen in Europe, even giraffes. It was said that he also kept Saracen dancing girls for his entertainment. At times Frederick claimed to be a skeptic who believed in none of the Church's teachings. He was certainly willing to oppose the Pope politically when necessary.

Much later he would break with the Pope completely, but at the moment he was still a Christian prince waiting to go on Crusade, and if he cared little for the spiritual benefits, he knew that fighting on the Pope's side would bring him political ones. But the rebellious cities continued to block their way to Cremona and prevented the Diet from opening. Ludwig joined the campaign against them, which kept him from Elizabeth for many months. It was the longest separation of their married life.

At home, three years of long winters, poor harvests, floods and pestilence were taking their toll. Famine swept through Germany. Many people, particularly the poorest, were dying. In Ludwig's absence, Elizabeth had to see to the welfare of her people.

Isentrude says that Elizabeth's husband had given her the *facultas*, that is, the authority to carry out anything "which pertained to the work and the honor of God, and promoting the salvation of souls." She judged that this was the perfect occasion to use it, for what was more a work of God than charity? She immediately began to feed all of the poor by seeing to the distribution of her husband's personal grain harvest in each of his four principalities. She personally took charge of the distribution of grain at the Wartburg. But there were many who were too ill and weak to come to the general distribution in front of the castle. For them, Elizabeth had a hospital built near Wartburg.

The founding and endowing of hospitals was a very common actity for rulers and nobility at the time. We find in the documents of Ludwig's reign that already in 1223, he had helped endow a hospital in Gotha, and had urged his people to contribute to it. In this case, the building had been donated by a woman named Hildegard. The document says: "We therefore make known to everyone who sees this instrument or hears its contents that we establish the house that Lady Hildegard in Gotha voluntarily makes available as a hospital, in complete agreement with our beloved mother and wife as well as our brothers. If anyone transfers houses or courtyards of the city (or) any income to this above-mentioned house for the redemption of his sins, waiving any revocation, we therefore confirm it for all time."[1] Part of the hospital building survives to this day.

The foundations of Elizabeth's new hospital were discovered during excavations carried out in 2006. The site is called "St. Elizabeth's Plain," a level place located to the northeast of the Wartburg, halfway down the steep descent between the castle and the town of Eisenach. Part of the Romanesque stone wall and the foundations survive. The dimensions were 23 feet wide and 32 feet in length. The upper part of the building, like most at the time, would have been of wood. It probably also had a chapel or at least a space with an altar.[2] It was near the site of a well or spring from which the castle drew its water, called St. Elizabeth's Well. The site was undoubtedly chosen because a hospital needed an abundant water supply nearby for sanitation.

Elizabeth tended the sick, even the worst cases, with her own hands. Isentrude describes this at great length. Elizabeth would wipe the filth from the mouths, ears and noses of the sick, and would not even notice the bad smells she ordinarily hated, even though her handmaids could not bear it. She gave special attention to the sickest and most wretched children, even the ones with the most disfiguring diseases; they had scabies and no doubt lice. Nevertheless, Elizabeth did not hesitate to embrace them. She even remembered to bring them playthings. She was so kind and affectionate that all the poor children would run to her and call her "mother." And she did all this with her ready and ever-present smile. Though Elizabeth did not realize it, this was the beginning of the work she would carry out later in Marburg, the hospital work that would make her renowned throughout the world.

Not satisfied with this, Elizabeth took much food out of her own mouth to feed the poor. She was so busy she had little time to care whether she ate or not. Her work for the poor occupied her day and night. And there were the usual state occasions and religious ceremonies, where she would fill in for Ludwig. And then she had to see that her own children were fed and cared for, and had to answer their persistent question: when was their father coming home? She must have been grateful to be so busy; it gave her less time to miss him.

She made sure not only that the weak were taken care of, but that those strong enough to work were fed until the new crop came in. Then she gave them clothes and shoes, so their feet would not be hurt by the grain stubble, and supplied them with scythes so they could gather the harvest and so live off the labor of their own hands.

According to tradition, Elizabeth founded a second hospital in 1226, this time in Eisenach itself. It was opposite the Georgentor – St. George's Gate – at the site of the present church of St. Anne. Though no known traces of this hospital survive, it has been commemorated with a plaque above the archway of the church, which is believed to have been the hospital chapel.[3]

It is certain, though, that Elizabeth carried out her aid work in Eisenach as well. She distributed her own fine clothes to the poor in the marketplace, where many of the townspeople must have been hurt by the lack of bread and other foodstuffs to sell at market; she urged the recipients not to use the fine things for luxuries, but to sell them for money to tend to their needs. One poor woman was so ecstatic on receiving her clothes that she actually fell to the ground, crying out that there had never been any greater joy in the world. Elizabeth was actually afraid she might be the cause of the poor woman's death. She urged all the poor to work hard and made sure they had what was necessary for them to do so.

Elizabeth saw each poor or sick or marginalized person she came across as a child of God, and a brother or sister of Christ. Because of this, each and every human life was precious to her; each of the poor, sick and handicapped was a person of unique dignity. As St. James, said: "Did not God choose those who are poor in the world to be rich in faith and heirs of the kingdom that he promised to those who love him? But you have dishonored the poor person (James 2:4-5)." She understood that not only the duty, but the right to work is one of the things most conducive to human dignity, and tried to make sure that all the poor had the means to do this.

Looking back at Elizabeth's understanding of poverty as it developed, and has been recounted in these chapters, some people will say that she saw the problem in a modern way. In way, this is true. Her view, like the Franciscans and those in the poverty movement of her time, represented a new development in the understanding of poverty. Christians had always believed that those who were blessed with wealth had a duty to the poor, and that it was even theft to withold aid from them, denying the poor the goods of creation that everyone had a right to. Medieval Christian rulers tirelessly endowed charity work for the poor, including hospices and hospitals.

The contribution of Elizabeth and others of her time was to look toward the actual causes of poverty, and in many cases, she identified them as coming from the greed or neglect and mismanagement of the rich and the rulers. André Vauchez has said Elizabeth's protest against the injustices in feudal society was a purely personal and moral one, not one that looked to carry out structural changes.[4] While it is true that Elizabeth most likely saw her personal mission as primarily the establishment of a society based on Christian fraternity, which she accomplished through her example, she certainly didn't neglect the need for structural change. Due to particular circumstances her views on the structures of government were expressed largely through protest, but in this situation, when she was given a free hand, we can perhaps see her ideas best.

One thing that strikes us is her sophisticated understanding of how the economy works. She was far-seeing enough to understand what many of the officials apparently did not: that the coming harvest was all-important to feed the whole country, and that if the ill or dying peasants could not work, no one would eat next year. She gave gave a well-balanced attention not just to government assistance to immediate needs, but to achieving a sound workforce and economic production that could itself contribute to the country's income.

Toward the end of the summer, Ludwig finally returned, to the great joy and relief of his family. Elizabeth was the happiest of all. She "welcomed her beloved with a thousand kisses pressed on him with her heart and her lips."[5] Elizabeth's grain distribution and work programs had been unpopular with the officials who counted only profits. The estate manager and steward wasted no time in coming to the Landgraf to criticize Elizabeth's activities during his absence. Something should be done to stop her. She would drain the whole treasury if she had a chance! And the Landgraf would suffer, as would, of course, his vassals. Ludwig's reaction was swift and firm: he ratified all of Elizabeth's decisions, and added: "Let her give for the sake of God and to benefit the poor all she wants, as long as she leaves the Neuenburg and Wartburg in my possession."[6] More than likely he had to suppress a smile at the thought of his wife giving his castles away too.

He had silenced the opposition to Elizabeth, but not for long.

❧

VII. The Crusader's Cross

The time for Ludwig's departure for the crusade came closer. Early in 1227, he received the cross again from Bishop Conrad of Hildesheim. Before his departure, as a sign of devotion and a reminder of the nature of the pilgrimage he was undertaking, he had a Passion play performed by clerics at the Wartburg. Some of those who witnessed it later told Caesarius of Heisterbach that they really felt they were gazing on the death of Christ with their own eyes.[1] Elizabeth herself must have watched it with overwhelming emotion. From time to time women took the cross as a sign of spiritual support for the Crusade: Elizabeth must have felt that she wore it already on her heart.

She was now pregnant with her third child, and at such a moment, the separation seemed especially hard. She and Ludwig decided that, as a thanksgiving for their life together, they would give their coming child to God. If it was a boy, he would be given as an oblate to the monastery of Ramerstorff, but if it was a girl, to Altenberg; both were Premonstratensian foundations.

Ludwig called all his knights and nobles together at Creuzburg castle and asked them to rule their lands peacefully and justly in his absence. He recalled the many wars of his father's day, and added: "God has granted to me as he did to Solomon the son of King David, peaceful and quiet times. And behold, all things are peaceful, because he himself grants peace.

But, for the sake of his charity and for our salvation, I am leaving behind my wife and children, along with my beloved brothers and my rich lands, along with my relatives and neighbors and friends and people at peace, and in God's name, I am going forth as a pilgrim. Therefore I ask all of you to pray that I may be restored whole to you, if in the end it is pleasing to His mercy, for I put myself, and you who are subject to me above all things, at the disposal of His most Serene Majesty."[2]

The Crusaders in the area planned to meet for their departure at Schmalkalden, near the border of Hesse, on June 24, 1227, the feast day of St. John the Baptist. Hundreds of knights gathered there at the appointed time, together with the bishop of Augsburg and other clergy, pilgrims, infantry, camp equipment, provender, and horse- and mule-drawn wagons. There Ludwig said goodbye to his family, with many tears on both sides. And then they were off, with banners flying. At the last moment, Elizabeth decided to ride part of the way with Ludwig. She traveled with him one day, then, because she couldn't tear herself away, a second; she was still with him when they crossed the borders of Thuringia.

Finally, Rudolph of Vargila, Ludwig's cupbearer, said to him: "My lord, it is time for your lady to return; it must be."

Ludwig took out a signet ring and showed it to Elizabeth; it had on it a relief of the Lamb of God with a banner. He told her that any message sealed with it could be trusted as coming from him, and seeing the ring itself, she would know that he was dead. He added, "May almighty God bless you, my dearest sister, and blessed be the fruit of your womb that you bear. Faithfully arrange about it as we have promised each other."[3]

Elizabeth embraced and kissed her husband for the last time, then remounted and rode home. From that moment on, she lived like a widow, but still in hope of his return.

Ludwig and his knights, along with clergy, bishops and pilgrims from all over Thuringia, Hesse and Saxony, rode south along the eastern coast of Italy, beside the sparkling blue Adriatic sea. They were heading for the heel of Italy, the port of Brindisi, where the crusaders were to embark for the Holy Land. The journey as far as Sicily took more than a month. The emperor Frederick himself came to meet them at Troia on August 3 and rode south with them. When they reached Brindisi, the summer's heat had begun to affect many of the northern travelers. Because of the huge press of crusaders and pilgrims, there was a severe shortage of food in the city. Frederick had fallen ill on the journey south and need time to recover, so they were forced to wait for their embarkation.

And then came the epidemic. Thousands of crusaders and pilgrims in the camps around Brindisi fell sick and many died.

It was a sad remnant of the original German company that finally set sail toward the end of August. But Ludwig stayed behind with Frederick to attend him during his recovery. Toward the end of their stay, Ludwig himself began to feel feverish, but nevertheless on September 9, they finally sailed from Brindisi. On the 10th they made port at Otranto, so Ludwig could pay his respects to the emperor's young wife Isabelle, who resided at his palace there. But by the time they returned to the ship, the Landgraf was gravely ill.

The course of the illness was swift. Ludwig asked for a priest. Gerold, the patriarch of Jerusalem, who was in Otranto at the time, came to administer the last rites and Viaticum to him. He brought with him as his assistant Cardinal Leo Brancaleone, whose titular church was Holy Cross in Jerusalem in Rome. Ludwig received the Last Sacraments devoutly. It soon became clear that death was imminent. Suddenly Ludwig stirred and turned to those present. "Do you see those white doves?" he asked. They believed him delirious.

After a little while, he murmured, "I must fly away with these most splendid doves." Shortly afterwards, he breathed his last. The chaplain Berthold, who recorded all this, saw some white doves flying to the east and followed them a wondering gaze.[4] It was September 11, 1227. Ludwig was just twenty-seven years old.

Back at the Wartburg, on September 29, Elizabeth gave birth to her third child, a daughter Gertrude. As she cared for her new baby, Elizabeth must have longed every day for a message from her husband. He must have sailed long ago, but perhaps he had been able to send word from Brindisi first. She counted the days: even the fastest messengers couldn't make the journey from Otranto to Eisenach in under a month, so it would probably take longer. But at length, around the middle or end of October, messengers did arrive, but not with the hoped-for assurance; instead the family learned that Ludwig was dead. They kept the news from Elizabeth at first, because she was still recovering from childbirth. Surprisingly, only one medieval source tells us in detail how Elizabeth received the news of her husband's death, and that is Dietrich of Apolda. He says that it was the Landgrafin Sophia herself—so long wrongly considered a heartless mother-in-law—who decided that she must be told as gently as possible. She left her monastery and came to the Wartburg, with some other noble ladies. With her she had Ludwig's signet ring, which the messengers had brought.

Elizabeth received them warmly. When she was seated, Sophia began, "Have courage my dear daughter, and do not be troubled about what the divine will has decreed in regard to your husband, my son."

Elizabeth must have been alarmed by their solemn manner. She must have guessed the truth, on seeing the ring, which Ludwig would never have sent during his lifetime; but in desperation, she seized on the best possible interpretation:

"If my brother is being held prisoner, with the help of God and our friends, he will be freed." Now there was no possible way to soften the blow:

"He is dead," Sophia said.

Elizabeth griped her knees with her knotted hands, trying to control herself. But she could not hold back a cry: "He is dead, dead, and the world and everything that is sweet in the world is dead to me!"

She jumped up and ran wildly through the length of the castle, stopping only when she ran into a wall. She clung there, sobbing until they pulled her away and took her to rest. Ludwig her comforter was gone, so all comfort was gone. Even God himself must have seemed absent, though, says Dietrich, the wise friar who recorded this scene, the Holy Spirit, the true comforter of souls, was still near her.[5]

❧

VIII. "Lord, I Want to

Be With You"

The Landgraf's family was united for a time in their grief, but problems arose that soon destroyed the united front and left Elizabeth homeless and in poverty with her three children. What happened is one of the most obscure and controversial parts of her life. But we can reconstruct it in some sense from the sources. My understanding of it departs in several instances from the common interpretations. A long-standing tradition holds that she was expelled by her husband's family from the Wartburg. On the other hand, most modern historians believe that she left her wealthy life under pressure by her husband's family, in order to be able to follow her conscience about unjust food and to devote herself to Franciscan poverty. But I am convinced that these interpretations are mistaken. (For more on the reasons for this, see the Appendix).

The events require some preliminary explanation. First, we must recall that Ludwig had given Elizabeth complete power in regard to charitable distribution of his property and that she had used that power to its fullest in his absence during the famine of 1226. In fact, Huyskens believed that she actually acted as regent during this time.[1] She had also been able to administer her dower properties on her own, which was a break from tradition for the wife of a living ruler in Thuringia. She would undoubtedly have enjoyed the same powers when Ludwig left for the crusade. Isentrude states more than once that many of the nobles and some of the Landgraf's family were outraged at Elizabeth's stand against the injustice of the tax policies and the fraud of the tax collectors, and perhaps the unjust acquisition of territory. And she had the power to implement her ideas. We also know that many of Ludwig's most faithful vassals had set off with him for the Holy Land. After his death, Elizabeth would have been without support. Many of the remaining vassals must have feared that if she were free to administer her dower lands herself, she would engage in even more ruinous spending of the income of the properties and interference with the taxes.

Elizabeth no doubt expected to continue administering her dower property, as she had done while married. It was the one way she could continue to obey her conscience in regard to unlawful food. Her brother-in-law, Heinrich Raspe, now acting as Landgraf and regent for Elizabeth's young son Hermann, would have found it difficult to oppose this: for a widow, it was the customary law.

It seems likely, though the sources do not directly state this, that Elizabeth left the Wartburg not long after her husband's death. With her children and her faithful ladies-in-waiting, she went to her dower property in Marburg. We don't know the date that she left, but most likely it was November or December of 1227. She would perhaps have needed to make some administrative decisions, and see for herself from close by how things were being governed. It would also have been a quiet place to stay while she grieved and decided how she was to live the life of continence she had promised to observe if her husband died.

Many have supposed, without very good reason, that Elizabeth desired to immediately embark on a life of Franciscan poverty. But this would have been an unlikely decision for the mother of three very small children. She might have decided to live much as before, in as penitential a life as she could, until the children were older and able to look after themselves before making her final choice of a way of life. If so, then God was to upset her plans and force a decision in an unexpected way.

Caesarius of Heisterbach gives us a clue to the developments that followed. He says that in determining how they acted toward Elizabeth, Heinrich Raspe and Ludwig's youngest brother Conrad, "who were still minors, were governed by the advice of the vassals and the *ministeriales*."[2] These were two different classes of knights; the first were the major vassals, or the landed nobles who regarded Ludwig as their lord. The class of *ministeriales* began in Germany as serfs who carried out administrative tasks for their lord; from the eleventh century onward they became a separate division of "unfree" knighthood and received fiefs, but for the most part they still carried out administrative functions. This last group would have included the tax collectors. Both the vassals and the *ministeriales* had reason to dislike Elizabeth; Caesarius' statement indicates that the opposition against her was widespread. Neither Heinrich nor Conrad was as strong in character as Ludwig had been; they were swayed where he could not be.

Isentrude, who was with Elizabeth throughout this whole period, tells us what happened next: "After her husband's death, Elizabeth was ejected from the castle and all the possessions of her dower by some of her husband's vassals, since her husband's brother was still young." Isentrude does try to excuse Heinrich, but though Elizabeth's enemies may have manipulated him, it is hard to imagine the offended vassals acting without his approval. So the armed men went to Marburg, with the mission of expelling Elizabeth from the castle and occupying it. From now on they would control and administer all of her property. Perhaps they had even been asked to take Elizabeth and the children into custody— for their own good, of course.

Could Elizabeth have expected such a development? She most likely would have had men-at-arms of her own to serve as protection, but perhaps they weren't able to resist so sudden an attack. She, her children and her little retinue were somehow able to flee down the steep hill from the castle to the town below. They must have feared that they would be pursued. And they could not go very fast: five-year-old Hermann and three-year old Sophia could not keep up with the adults for long and had to be carried. Elizabeth held baby Gertrude in her arms. By now, it was winter, and as Isentrude recalls, bitterly cold. Evening was coming on. They slipped into the courtyard of an innkeeper and took refuge in a shed in which he kept his pigs. In spite of the terrible situation and the fear they must have felt, Elizabeth seemed to be joyful. She was now suffering something real for God.

Sometime after midnight, when the town was quiet, they decided to risk emerging from their hiding place. It was the hour for Matins. Elizabeth led the others to a place she knew she would be welcome: the little foundation of her friends, the Friars Minor. When they arrived at the church, the friars were already gathered to sing their office. Perhaps they had already heard what had happened, and were wondering where the Landgrafin had gone after her escape. Elizabeth asked them to add the singing of the *Te Deum laudamus* to their prayers, in thanksgiving to God for her tribulation. Did she recall what St. Francis had said about perfect joy lying in suffering for God's sake?[3]

The next day, Elizabeth went to the homes of the nobles and the rich people she knew in town, hoping one of them would take them in. But no one dared. They feared the new occupiers of the land. So the church of the friars became their shelter, for the tiny convent would have been too small to hold them, even if it had not been forbidden for women to be inside the cloister of a male monastery. But they could take comfort in the fact that churches were always places of sanctuary from violence.

They shivered with cold in the unheated place and tried to keep the children occupied. They could attend the friars' Mass and office. Still, they would not be able to stay there for long. Yet Elizabeth could not imagine where to lay her children's heads. No one would shelter the little ones who would one day inherit the land. This was the part Isentrude was most indignant about.

At last, Elizabeth went to the home of a priest, and by begging him to have mercy on her children, obtained shelter. But they were not able to stay there for long. Elizabeth's enemies eventually caught up with her and ordered her into one of their homes. It was a large residence, but she and her retinue were confined in a small space. We don't know how long she remained there or exactly how or why she was released. The following is speculation, but I think it is well-founded.

Heinrich Raspe may have given his original orders to expel Elizabeth simply because he felt sure she would return to the Wartburg once she was forced from her dower property. He may have been surprised when she did not return on her own, but he had underestimated her. She knew that she would be obliged to once again go hungry or act against her conscience in regard to food if she did come back. If she suspected Heinrich's treachery, she would have been even more reluctant to return. He sent word for the vassals to take her into custody. Nevertheless, he would not have wanted to use more force than necessary. Her custodians were to try to persuade her to return voluntarily. When she proved stubborn, Heinrich grew alarmed; Elizabeth may have been disliked by some of the nobility, but she was immensely popular among many other people, and could rally a large number of them to her cause. It may have taken weeks for messages to go back and forth between Marburg and Eisenach, but eventually Heinrich gave orders to free her.

Whatever the case may have been, Elizabeth, her children and her ladies were released. It is here that we have the only expression approaching bitterness we will hear from Elizabeth. As they left, she thanked the walls that had sheltered her, and added: "I would gladly thank the people, but I don't know why." They went back to their poor dirty shelter; Isentrude doesn't say whether this was the shed with the pigs or the priest's house. But it seems almost unimaginable that they could have stayed in the first of these places for long.

Elizabeth was evidently no longer disturbed or threatened. But because of her poverty, she eventually had to relinquish custody of her children. She would not return to the Wartburg herself. But Heinrich Raspe would not have accepted the idea of the heir to Thuringia and his sisters living in a hovel. Let Elizabeth stay there if she wanted to, but the children would have to come home. Though Isentrude doesn't say so—she only mentions that they were sent to "distant places"—they must have been taken back to the Wartburg or Creuzberg.

During this time of suffering and hunger, Elizabeth paradoxically no longer felt abandoned by God. One day, she was so weak as she knelt in church that she had to lean against the wall. But she kept her eyes fixed constantly on the altar. Isentrude, who was with her, felt that she must be having one of her mystical experiences. On returning to her poor hovel, Elizabeth ate a little food, but then became so faint she had to lean against the wall. She fell and Isentrude caught her in her arms. Everyone else was sent out, and Isentrude sat with her.

After a time, Elizabeth, who was looking toward the window, opened her eyes and began to laugh gently. After a time, she closed her eyes and wept. She continued to alternate between tears and laughter until Compline, when after a period of silence she suddenly said, "So then, Lord, you want to be with me and I want to be with you and I never want to be separated from you." When she came back to herself, and Isentrude asked her who she had been talking to, she answered: "I saw the heavens open and sweet Jesus my Lord bending down toward me and consoling me for the many difficulties and tribulations which surrounded me, and when I saw him, I was filled with joy and I laughed. But when he turned his face away, as if he were about to withdraw, I wept. Taking pity on me, he again turned his most serene face towards me, saying, 'If you want to be with me, I will be with you.'" And it was then, she explained, that she had spoken as she had done. At last Elizabeth had from God the answer to her difficulties; at last she was fully united to him.

Isentrude asked Elizabeth to tell her about the previous vision she had experienced in church when the host was raised, evidently referring to the church visit she had just made, but Elizabeth would not do so. She said: "It is better not to reveal what I saw there, but you should know that I was in the greatest joy, and I saw wonderful secrets of God."

During those days, Elizabeth suffered what many women do because of poverty. She worried about finding enough food for her children and where they would sleep. Eventually she was even forced to give up custody of them. This was poverty in a very different sense than the poverty chosen by religious, the one that was generally regarded as meritorious in the eyes of the devout. Actual poverty was still looked down on. But this poverty was God's providence for Elizabeth. If she had not been forced into it, she might not have been able to take the last step God was demanding of her. At the moment she said to Jesus, "I never want to be separated from you," she must have known that she could not turn back. She was going to live wholly for him, united to his sufferings.

Evidently feeling that there was no hope of dealing with her brothers-in-law, Elizabeth turned to her mother's German relatives. She found her way to her mother's sister, Mechtild, the abbess of the Benedictine abbey of Kitzingen in Franconia, some days' journey away. Mechtild was ready to help, and took her to her brother, and Elizabeth's uncle, Eckbert, the bishop of Bamberg. He received her kindly, and seemed intent on helping her solve her difficulty. But when Elizabeth learned how he was going to do so, she was alarmed. He advised her that she could find a safe haven by marrying again. He explained that her previous vow to remain continent in the event of her husband's death should be looked on as conditional, an idea which Elizabeth vehemently rejected. Even if it hadn't been repugnant to her to accept any other man after Ludwig, nothing would induce her to go against her vow. Her uncle, no longer so kindly, began to insist.

Guda and Isentrude, who had taken the vow of continence with her, feared that he would try to force her to remarry and that they would have to live their life of continence alone. But Elizabeth reassured them: "I did not make this vow on condition that it please my friends or provided that God did not reveal some other plan to me—I vowed absolutely [to preserve] total continence after my husband's death." She added: "If I had no other way of escaping, I would cut off my nose in secret. No one would trouble any more about me if I were frightfully mutilated like that." In the end, her uncle had her taken to a castle he owned, called Pottenstein, on the Püttlach river in Upper Franconia, to stay until she came to her senses. In short, though our source, Isentrude, doesn't say so directly, Elizabeth was once again in prison. But this time, in a sense, it would be Ludwig who would rescue her.

꙰

IX. The Beloved Bones

The knights who had accompanied Ludwig on his crusade had learned about his death through messengers before they had been long at sea; they had returned and buried their lord temporarily before continuing to the Holy Land to fulfill their vow. But they went without their leader, the Emperor Frederick. On September 29, 1227, Pope Gregory IX, angry at the emperor's continued delays on starting out, had excommunicated him. Frederick would not return to the Pope's good graces and depart for the east until June 28, 1228. So Ludwig's vassals must have satisfied themselves with seeing those holy sites the Muslims had not banned from Christian visits before heading home.

When they came ashore in Otranto, they exhumed the Landgraf's body from its temporary burial place and started on their long, sad journey to Thuringia. They placed his bones in caskets and strapped them to a mule, topped with a jeweled silver cross. After every day's journey, they would stop for the night at a local church, and the clergy and faithful would keep vigil over the remains. In the morning, the priests would say Mass, and the faithful knights would pray for Ludwig's soul. It must have been sometime in March 1228 when they reached Bamberg. When Bishop Eckbert heard of their arrival, he sent a message to Elizabeth at Pottenstein castle, and she was released so she could go to Bamberg to honor her husband's remains. The bishop himself, with many of the clergy, religious and nobility of the city, went in procession to meet the returning knights with their burden. Then they went on to the cathedral, singing hymns. The bells of the churches rang out, and people flowed in from everywhere.

At the cathedral, Elizabeth was there, to the surprise of the vassals, for they would not have expected to see her so far from home. The procession entered by the Romanesque portal and continued down the nave. At the altar, the caskets were unlocked and the cloths unwrapped from the bones. Isentrude recalls vividly what happened as those gathered were preparing to sing the Office of the Dead. Anyone who was in church that day would scarcely have been able to forget it. As Elizabeth knelt by her husband's bones and wept, she began to pray out loud: "Lord, I give you thanks for having mercifully consoled me by these bones of my husband which I have so much desired. Great as my love for him was, you know that I do not begrudge the sacrifice that my beloved and I made of himself to you for the liberation of the Holy Land. If I could have him, I would give the whole world for him, and go begging with him forever. But I call upon you to witness that I would not want to redeem his life, even if it cost me but a single hair, if it were against your will. Now I recommend myself and him to your grace. May your will for us be done."

In the past, her dream had been that she would be able to fulfill her wish to live a life of poverty, even of begging, and to still have Ludwig with her. He was the one thing she would have had difficulty in giving up to God, the one thing she might have been tempted to grudge him. But she was speaking the truth: she accepted the sacrifice as God's will for her. When he heard this, even the bishop must have been brought to understand that Elizabeth would never marry again after such a love, and with that kind of faith.

When the ceremony in the cathedral was over, Elizabeth was at leisure to greet her husband's faithful vassals. She went with them to the nearby meadow, and sat with them gathered around her. She knew that her future depended on what she said now. She spoke to them graciously and told them everything that had happened, not omitting the indignities she had suffered, ending, no doubt, with her treatment by the bishop. Bishop Eckbert began to look uncomfortable. Elizabeth won the complete support of these vassals, and some dark looks were no doubt exchanged between them and the bishop. After consultation with the knights and receiving their assurance that they would look after her interests, the bishop entrusted her to their care. (Or such was the polite language in which the chroniclers couched it).

Elizabeth, now free, accompanied her husband's body home to Thuringia, where with the most magnificent ceremonies, he was buried in the monastery of Reinhardsbrunn.

It seemed that Elizabeth's problems might now be solved at last. Nevertheless, says Isentrude, everyone neglected her interests and she lived in poverty as before. Or at least, as Dietrich of Apolda has it, Ludwig's vassals reproached her brothers-in-law, Heinrich Raspe and Conrad, who said that of course they would welcome her at the Wartburg, living on the *sustentatio*, or common family revenues, until the matter of her dower property could be resolved.[1] But she would not consent to more than a short visit. She disdained living at court, because, as the witness Irmingard later recalled: "she did not want to receive her nourishment by theft and by taxing the poor, as was so often the practice at the courts of princes." She may also have believed that Heinrich's promises to restore her dowry were empty ones, and that his real aim was to get her to come back to her previous life and forget her scruples.

The Anonymous Franciscan tells us that the friars had advised Elizabeth to trust to Master Conrad's advice, but either his intervention was unsuccessful, or he was absent on another preaching tour. Perhaps Elizabeth stayed at this time near the monastery of Reinhardsbrunn, where she could freely visit her husband's tomb and find some comfort there.

In fact, a story about this period was preserved by the monks of the place that indicates that this was the case. While visiting her husband's tomb at the monastery, and dressed in her poor clothes, Elizabeth met a lay brother of lowly birth named Volkmar, who served as miller at the monastery, and "quickly extended charity and communion by holding out her hand, and accepted from the man, although he resisted, his humble pledge of fraternity. For the good peasant blushed at touching the hand of that most illustrious and holy woman." The monks also recorded that after Elizabeth moved to Marburg, the brother's hand, the one with which he had pledged fraternity to her, was crushed in the mill works and refused to heal. On the night she died, Elizabeth appeared to brother Volkmar, and again taking his hand, healed it.[2]

In Rome, Pope Gregory IX had heard about Elizabeth's difficulties. A messenger soon arrived with papal letters appointing Conrad of Marburg as her protector and taking her and her goods under the spiritual protection of the Holy See. This put an end to the persecution against her and finally prevailed on her brothers-in-law to change their minds about returning her dower.

Until recently, historians did not know who had appealed to Rome on Elizabeth's behalf to obtain these letters. Now we know through the newly-recovered testimony of a Franciscan friar, Brother Andrew of Westphalia, that he himself had made his way to Rome to appeal to the Holy See on her behalf. He may have come to know Elizabeth because he had been one of the clergy in the entourage of Frederick II. He had studied canon law, perhaps at the famous University of Bologna, and was no doubt familiar with the Curia. On his arrival, he approached his good friend and former schoolmate, Cardinal Leo Brancaleone, on her behalf. This now-aged prelate had been a trusted legate of Pope Innocent III in many difficult negotiations. He was not only a diplomat, however, but a great friend of St. Francis and his order. He was also the very cardinal who had given Ludwig the last rites in Otranto. He readily obtained the letters from the Pope that would restore Elizabeth's property to her. On receiving them, the vassals who had been persecuting her had no more power, and Elizabeth's brothers-in law had to restore her property.

But by this time, Elizabeth no longer wanted possessions, because she had decided she wanted to live a religious life. Heinrich and Conrad gave her a cash indemnity for most of her dower, which she wanted to give to the poor, and returned to her only a small part of the original property.

Now Elizabeth was free to follow her desire for a life wholly dedicated to God. She conferred with Master Conrad about what form that life should take. Should she enter the Cistercians, and follow the mitigated form of the rule, as her mother-in-law had? Join another religious order or become a recluse or anchoress? Or follow the life of the Beguines, who lived as "sisters in the world," but without vows? For Elizabeth, her life had to be the most perfect one possible. While Conrad weighed the possibilities, Elizabeth brought up the way of life she wanted above all: to live like the rest of the poor, indeed to beg from door to door as Francis himself had wanted his friars to do. She told Conrad this, and he reacted with a categorical "no." This was far too controversial and dangerous a way of life for a woman to live—even though she had already been forced to beg from door to door for shelter, had suffered from extreme poverty, and had been constantly mocked and ridiculed by her enemies! Elizabeth begged him tearfully, but he was adamant. Finally, she said, "I will do this, for you can't forbid me." Bowing at last to her conscience and necessity, Conrad agreed to at least let her make her complete renunciation of the world and binding vow of continence as soon as possible, even though she did not yet enter any order. Most likely Elizabeth wanted to do this to prevent any more attempts to force her into another marriage. This time her vows would be unequivocal.

On Good Friday, March 24, 1228, the Landgraf's family, including the children, assembled at the chapel that Elizabeth had given the Franciscans in Eisenach, where the altar had been stripped bare in honor of Christ's passion. In the presence of some of the friars, Elizabeth put her hands on the altar and, as Conrad says, "renounced her own will, all the pomp of the world, and everything that the Savior of the world counsels us to forsake in his Gospel"—that is, she vowed to renounce the world and follow the evangelical counsels of poverty, chastity and obedience. There is no mention in Conrad's bare account of the ceremony of Elizabeth putting on a habit or being tonsured. This was because she did not profess a definite form of religious life. Nevertheless, her vows of continence and obedience to Conrad would have put her into the penitent state, which was regarded as a religious state by medieval theologians and canon law. Conrad was still in favor of her living in a convent and he must certainly have let her know that she had to be prepared to follow this course in obedience if he ordered it.[3]

The vow that Elizabeth most desired to take was one of poverty. But this presented a problem. She wanted to renounce all her possessions, but Conrad would not allow her to do so, because she needed to pay her husband's debts and continue to give to the poor. Her mother-in-law Sophia had received a dispensation to follow a mitigated form of poverty for the same reason—to compensate for any wrong or fraud that her husband might have been responsible for in his lifetime, and to pay anything he owed to anyone.

Now Elizabeth's soul had at last achieved peace. She felt she belonged completely to God. But her future way of life was still uncertain.

X. The Hospital in Marburg

Shortly after this, Elizabeth received a letter from Pope Gregory IX, giving her advice about her choice of a form of religious life. He wrote of his joy at hearing how "you so ardently desire to bear the marks of Our Lord's passion." But he also cautioned her not to be rash in her choice, and not to leave the contemplative life for the active life until it had strengthened her: Sit often with Mary at the feet of the Savior, so that you may delight in the graceful words that flow from his mouth. Submit your spiritual desires to examination: do not let anything of vice be hidden in them under the veil of virtue, and immediately exclude from your mind whatever might be an obstacle to your conscience and reputation. . . . Do not cease praying, do not leave the feet of the Lord, until the southern breeze blows through the garden of your mind and inflames your soul to virtue in the face of supreme love.[1]

So now, in the spring and summer of 1228, Elizabeth had an important decision to make. After some reflection, she decided to build a hospital in Marburg and form a religious community to serve it. It was a natural development for her, since she had already given much time as Landgrafin to caring for the poor in the hospital she had founded in Eisenach. There were things that had to be done first. Because the nobles of Marburg and the area around it were still hostile toward her, Elizabeth and her household went to a small village nearby to stay until the hospital was completed. There she set up a makeshift dwelling for them in an abandoned and apparently roofless house, in a room with a hearth. Elizabeth made a roof with leafy branches, and when it rained, they found some shelter under the stairs. But they were often tormented by the heat of the sun, the storm winds and the smoke from the wood fire Elizabeth tried to cook on. But there was one overwhelming consolation: she was able to have her youngest child Gertrude, now a year and a half old, with her, for a short time before she had to give her up to the monastery of Altenberg.

Isentrude tells us that it was only at this time that Elizabeth was finally able to make the most difficult renunciation that Master Conrad required of her as part of his campaign to have her regard all earthly things with contempt: he urged her to renounce her love for her children. Elizabeth obediently prayed for this, and later told her handmaids that God had heard her prayer: "As God is my witness, I am no longer worried about my children. I love them as I love any other neighbor. I have entrusted them to God; let him do with them as he wills."

This is the one aspect of Elizabeth's life that people have the most difficulty with. That she was forced to relinquish custody of her children is one thing, and is understandable, but that she seemingly became indifferent toward them is another. But when her words are understood properly, they show real wisdom. Elizabeth had to leave her children's future in God's hands, for her peace of mind and their good. She still loved them as her neighbors—and when we think of the intensity with which Elizabeth habitually loved "any other neighbor," we can be sure that her children did not lack her love. And it was necessary to keep them safe from the hardship and disease she would face in the hospital, at least until they were grown up and could decide for themselves if they wanted to live that life with her.

Pope Gregory IX approved of Elizabeth's choice to serve the sick. She had asked that the hospital be named for St. Francis, so he sent her a relic of the blood from the wound in the saint's side for the altar in the chapel, and granted an indulgence to the hospital in a bull dated April 19, 1229. This was one of the first foundations dedicated to the newly canonized Poverello.[2]

Finally the day came when Elizabeth was to profess and put on the habit in the Franciscan friary in Marburg, along with her handmaids Guda and Isentrude. Isentrude indicates that this took place more than a year after Ludwig's death. Since Elizabeth's daughter Gertrude was a year and a half old at the time she was living in the country village, this would put the profession sometime after the end of March 1229. But it is unlikely to have taken place much after April 19, the date of the Pope's indulgence, for the hospital would have been open by that time.

According to the Anonymous Franciscan, Brother Burchard, the Franciscan guardian of Hesse, tonsured Elizabeth and clothed her in the grey habit while Master Conrad said Mass. Another friar, Henry, called Placido, also witnessed the event. This was clearly a Franciscan profession. But in precisely what order was Elizabeth professed? Her life was an active one, unlike that of St. Clare and her sisters, who lived in enclosure. And the *Memoriale Propositi*, the primitive rule of the Franciscan Third Order, was intended for those living in the world in their homes, not for religious.

Many of the features of the active life of Elizabeth and her sisters were like that of the Beguines, groups of women who lived in loosely-structured communities, tending the sick or engaging in other works of the active life. Many of them were affiliated with male Franciscan communities. But Beguines did not make profession or take formal vows. Elizabeth has often been called the first Franciscan woman religious of the Third

Order. This is not quite accurate, for the rule and constitutions for the Third Order for religious did not yet exist. But her profession, unique for its time, can still be seen as the beginning of religious life in the Third Order.

The Anonymous Franciscan fondly recalls that from that time on, Elizabeth "walked with [the friars] in the house of God in perfect harmony." The hospital was very near the friary, though the friars were apparently not involved in running it. Two other woman also became her sisters, either now or later. Irmingard, by her own testimony, was of poor and humble birth. Like the other women at the hospital she wore the gray habit. The other was named Elisabeth; she was very likely of poor birth too. Both remained with Elizabeth at the hospital until her death.

Guda and Isentrude had expected all along to live their religious lives with Elizabeth; they had been through too much with her ever to leave her. But Master Conrad had other plans. He announced that they were to be separated from Elizabeth and live their vocations elsewhere. He did not want them to be able to speak with Elizabeth of the days of her past glory—and perhaps her past love. That was all over now. This was one of the hardest blows of all. But Elizabeth did not dare disobey Conrad's orders. There were many tears on both sides as Guda and Isentrude left; after this they only visited Elizabeth for brief periods.

Once the hospital was built, Elizabeth appointed a day when she would give what remained to her away to the poor, who were gathered together in the hospital courtyard. When everything had been distributed, she had a bonfire lit, and served the people bread; she even saw to washing and oiling their feet. The poor people, restored spiritually and physically, began to sing. Elizabeth said to her companions "You see, I told you we must make people happy," and rejoiced with them. She wanted to remove the social barriers between rich and poor.

Elizabeth and her sisters began their work at a time that marked a new phase in the development of hospitals in Europe. Most earlier hospital foundations had been attached to monasteries; in the thirteenth century, more and more hospitals in Germany were founded by confraternities in cities and towns. It was also the time when the military orders, which dedicated themselves to serving the sick as well as to fighting, established a number of hospitals in Germany, especially the Order of the Hospital of St. John of Jerusalem and the Teutonic order. Often men and women both served at the same hospital, but lived in separate quarters to preserve chastity. In the Teutonic Order, the noblewomen were called *consorores*, and the lay sisters who did the heavy work were called *conversae*. The women of the Premonstratensian order not only ran their own hospices but often tended to the sick in their homes.

From the few early documents dealing with Elizabeth's hospital, it seems to have been much like most of the hospitals run by confraternities in Germany in the thirteenth century. The director of the hospital was a layman named Hermann, whose wife Irmentrude also served the sick.[3] Some of the work was done by lay brothers; one of them, named Heinrich, served as Elizabeth's steward or manager. Then there were Elizabeth and the sisters, Irmingard and Elisabeth, and later Hildegunde, who served the sick with her. They lived a common life, but were not bound to complete poverty. Elizabeth earned extra money for herself and her sisters by spinning wool.

From this time on, Elizabeth gave herself entirely to the service of God's poor. She would bathe the sick and put them to bed, bind their sores and prepare their medicines. She was especially devoted to caring for the young children, including a little leper girl, whom she took to her own little house, talking to her and playing with her. She put the sickest and poorest at her own table.

Though there are no reliable statistics on the question, infanticide and abortion were certainly common practices in the Middle Ages, and Elizabeth was aware of the danger. She was always especially attentive to young mothers and mothers-to-be.

Once while she was staying in the village of Wetter, Elizabeth cared for a pregnant woman, arranging shelter for her in a shed next to her house, and caring for her for four weeks after the birth. When the woman was ready to leave, Elizabeth gave her some flour, bacon and lard, money and new clothes, and had Elisabeth, the sister who testified about it, remove her fur sleeves to wrap the child in. The woman's husband also received some shoes (there is no explanation for where he was during her pregnancy). Very early the next morning, the woman and her husband left secretly, abandoning the child in the house where she had stayed. Elizabeth called on the city magistrate to look for the parents, but to no avail. Shortly afterwards, however, the baby's father did return and confess, indicating that he had been unable to go on, and had returned as if by force. The mother confessed the same when she was found and begged forgiveness. The bystanders insisted that the woman be punished by having the clothes Elizabeth had given her taken away. Elizabeth said, "Do what you think is right." The clothes were taken away, but Elizabeth, taking pity on the woman, immediately gave her some other clothes. She showed a great deal more compassion on the woman than anyone else, perhaps because she knew what it was like to be led by circumstances to give up her children.

Sister Irmingard, who was of humble birth herself, was puzzled by this noblewoman who had chosen poverty and a little suspicious about her motives, as the poor sometimes are about the rich. She recalls how Elizabeth did not want to be called "Lady" by the sisters of humble background, but the familiar *Du* (Thou) or just "Elizabeth."

82

She would even have them sit next to her and eat from the same dish, a sign of familiarity. One day Irmingard said to her, "You acquire merit for yourself through us, but you don't pay any attention to our misfortune, that we might become proud because we are eating with you and sitting beside you." Elizabeth, in her usual playful way, replied: "Well, then, *thou* must sit in my lap," and she made Irmingard sit in her lap. Nor did Irmingard fully understand Elizabeth's spiritual views. In the hospital, when Elizabeth was bathing the poor and covering them with linen cloth, she said to Irmingard: "How good for us, that we can bathe and cover Our Lord in this way." Irmingard answered: "Good for us when we do things like this? I don't know if others feel like this."

We learn much less about the handmaid Elisabeth. She was evidently quiet and timid, though quite observant. She disliked Conrad and was afraid of him. She too found it difficult to use the familiar "Thou" for Elizabeth, and always called her "my lady" until the day of the saint's death. Conrad was gone more and more often on preaching tours. In order to make sure Elizabeth obeyed his orders, he had two of her household spy on her. He describes them as "a religious virgin of very low birth, and a noble widow, who was deaf and very severe." Some have thought that these were Irmingard and Elisabeth. This seems unlikely, for both of them seemed to dislike Conrad. Nevertheless, his absence left Elizabeth more freedom to visit with the friars at the hospital.

One of them, Gerard from beyond the Alps, recalled at her canonization process that "she commonly went about in a shabby tunic, patched, especially in the sleeves, girded with a quite rough cord, covered with a mantle that was patched in many places and lengthened with cloth of another color, like another abbess Clare of the cloistered sisters." The friars must have seen a likeness between Elizabeth and Clare not only in their habits but in their souls: both were deeply inclined to mystical union with God. In fact, Master Conrad wrote to the Pope: "In spite of these works of the active life, I declare before God that I have rarely seen a more contemplative woman." Conrad recalled that there were times when men and women religious saw Elizabeth coming from prayer, and seemed to see sunbeams coming from her eyes. Beyond this he says very little about Elizabeth's mystical life; perhaps she confided little about it to him. This would make her very different from other medieval female mystics, whose relationships with their confessors gave rise to spiritual confidences and recordings of their mystical experiences, as in the case of Catherine and Siena and her confessor, Brother Raymond of Capua.

Everything that Conrad reports about Elizabeth's mystical life, on the other hand, is secondhand. His whole plan for her spiritual development was indeed directed toward detaching her from the world and uniting her to God, but his approach seems more based on bringing her to God through obedience and fear rather than love. But even Isentrude, who was closer to Elizabeth than anyone, says very little about the secrets of her soul. For instance, she was able to recount only one mystical experience that Elizabeth revealed to her.

But one of the Franciscan brothers at the convent in Marburg, Gerard of Geldern, who was Elizabeth's confessor while Master Conrad was absent, seems to have known as much or more about her mystical life than anyone. The Anonymous Franciscan says that Gerard was more intimate with her and had more influence on her than anyone but Conrad.

Gerard was certainly qualified by his own temperament and interests to understand Elizabeth's mystical life. Geldern, a town in North Rhine-Westphalia in Germany, was near the territory of Brabant, where there were many women mystics at the time. In later years, at the friary in Regensburg, he would be part of the circle around the well-known Franciscan mystic David of Augsburg. Not only this, but as provincial minister of Upper Germany from around 1246 to 1252, Gerard would encourage one of his friars, Lamprecht von Regensburg, to write a mystical treatise called *Tochter Syon* (Daughter of Zion). Lamprecht even said that Gerard was the true author of the work: "From his mouth he gave me its subject matter and its sense."[4] The allegorical German poem describes how the soul looks for her true beloved through the intermediary of *Minne*, or Lady Love, a shining figure beloved of medieval mystical writers. She is based on the *Minne* or exalted love of the Minnesingers. It is Love who leads the soul to the King of Heaven and fires her arrows, like Cupid, into his breast, which create a wound, the blood of which refreshes his beloved. At last Christ and the soul are married with Love's help. To Gerard and Lamprecht, "Lady Love" was both the love that led Christ to suffer and the love that inspires the Christian soul to love him in return.[5]

Gerard may actually have become interested in mysticism from knowing Elizabeth. It is comforting to think that after the harshness she had experienced from Conrad of Marburg, Elizabeth finally may have found in Brother Gerard a kindred soul to direct her in the way of mystical love. The allegorical language of the mystical poets of the time seems rather far from Elizabeth's simple directness of expression. She had grown up with the poetry of the Minnesingers at court, but she showed little inclination to imitate their language. Nevertheless, the experiences the language tries to grasp are the same.

One day, Brother Gerard and Elizabeth were talking together at the hospital about the "priceless treasure of precious poverty," the subject so dear to St. Francis. How, they wondered, could it best be practiced? Elizabeth already seemed to be in ecstasy as she declared: "Since it is a question about holy poverty for me, I desire with all my heart that at the crossroads outside the walls a cell should be made for me of muddy straw and earth, and that in front of the little door or window a linen thread should be tied, and a small container hung on it, in which passersby would put alms to sustain me in a transitory way, as it is customary to do for poor lepers." So saying, she fell into ecstasy— and, just as in the ecstasy that Isentrude witnessed, Gerard caught her in his arms as she fell. He stayed with her until she revived and began to praise God. It is hard to imagine a more Franciscan scene than this; it is worthy of the *Fioretti*. For Elizabeth as for Francis, poverty was the thing that brought her closest to God.

This story also indicates that Elizabeth still desired a life of begging, and even seemed to have devised a way she might be able to achieve it without going from door to door, which Conrad had forbidden. Yet she had not chosen to live the life of a recluse, but a life of service. She described her life to Irmingard as that of the "sisters in the world," those like the Beguines who were the most despised of religious, because they did not follow the norm for women of being cloistered. The word used for Elizabeth's companions in religious life is *ancille*, or handmaids; it was applied not only to the noble Guda and Isentrude, but to the poor sisters Elisabeth and Irmingard as well. In fact, Conrad uses it for Elizabeth herself. It was not merely a term indicating that the women served Elizabeth, but a religious term describing the life of service they wanted to lead.[6] It had a clear Biblical precedent in the words of the Virgin Mary to the angel Gabriel, *Ecce ancilla Domini*, or "Behold the handmaid of the Lord," in which she agreed to do God's will in becoming the mother of Jesus (Luke 1:38). A number of medieval religious women, including some who were wealthy and noble, chose to call themselves handmaids in order to express their desire to be absolutely abject in their humility and obedience to God.

Elizabeth and her sisters lived together in the same house, and Elizabeth shared equally in the lowliest tasks. Irmingard tells how the saint would wash the earthenware dishes and utensils they used, and often sent the others off on errands so they could not prevent her from doing so. When they returned they would find her hard at work washing the dishes.

The Anonymous Franciscan says that Elizabeth longed to be able to live in the same way as the friars, who were free to be completely poor and go begging. He recalls her saying, "If God, the creator of all, had seen fit to create me a man, I would have worked faithfully with all my strength to give myself back to him as a Friar Minor!" But she quickly added, "I protest before angels and men that in this vale of misery, I desire nothing else to be made of me, a miserable sinner, except what the will of divine clemency will think it fitting to arrange."[7] She was well aware that a woman in her time was much more limited in her choices than a man, but she did not let it stop her from accomplishing great things.

Other women also imitated Elizabeth's way of life. Brother Gerard from beyond the Alps recalled that a noblewoman, a relative of Emperor Frederick II, wore the same dress as Elizabeth, and even begged from the friars. These were the first of many women to imitate Elizabeth through the centuries, and to forge new religious paths for women that she was only able to dream of.

During the last two or three years of her life, Elizabeth was often ill. But illness did not discourage her or keep her from dedicating herself constantly to her poor. Even when forced to go to bed, she would spin wool. When Irmingard took the distaff from her so she wouldn't tire herself, she would spread out and prepare the wool with her hands. From time to time she consulted a doctor so that her illness would not impede her from God's service. Yet she still seemed relatively healthy at the beginning of November 1231. Master Conrad was suffering from a severe illness himself at the time and believed he would die. He was anxious to know what Elizabeth's plans for her future life were when he was gone. But Elizabeth told him she would die before him. In fact, four days later, she fell ill. The nature of her illness is unknown; there are no real clues in the sources. Some think her health may have been harmed by childbearing at a very young age. It is also possible that her body was simply worn out from her privations, or that she was even infected with one of the illnesses that the people she nursed suffered from.

The witnesses of her final illness describe her as being cheerful and deeply absorbed in prayer. She told her sisters that she felt no pain, only weakness. Three days before her death she excluded all lay people from her bedside because "she wanted to mediate on her end, and the severe judgment of the dead and her omnipotent judge." But she did have beside her a little boy she had cured of scabies. As he played by her bedside, did her thoughts turn to her own children?

XI. The Glory of Heaven

On Sunday, November 16, very early in the morning, after the singing of Matins, it was clear she might not last the day. It was time for the last preparations for death to be made. Conrad heard her last confession and gave her Communion. He asked what she wanted done with her belongings, and she answered that everything that seemed to belong to her even a short time before was the property of the poor and should be given to them. We are reminded of St. Francis as he lay dying, desiring perfect poverty. She kept only the simple tunic in which she was dressed and in which she asked to be buried.

Her own religious sisters and some other men and women religious were beside her; the Franciscans of the community near the hospital were surely at her bedside too. During her illness, in answer to the request of her steward, Brother Heinrich, who wanted to become a Franciscan, she had spoken to the friars on his behalf; they had willingly received him into the order. She spent the day growing weaker but absorbed in meditation, and recalled to those around her how Christ wept at the raising of Lazarus.

When the religious around her wept, she showed a little of her old spirit, saying: "Daughters of Jerusalem, weep not for me, but for yourselves." At that moment, she seemed to be identifying herself with Christ on the way to Calvary. Then she fell silent, and lay turned toward the wall. After a while, those who were standing by heard sweet heavenly voices, as though they were all coming from her throat.

She turned and spoke to one of the handmaids, Elisabeth: "Where are you, dear?"

The sister said, "Here I am," and added, "Oh, my lady, how sweetly you sing."

Elizabeth said, "I tell you that between me and the wall, a little bird was singing very merrily, and I was so stirred by its voice that I had to sing too."

Was she thinking of the doves Ludwig had seen at his death? Or of the birds that attended St. Francis at his death?

Midnight was approaching, traditionally believed to be the hour when the Virgin gave birth, the hour of the dawn of our redemption. Elizabeth seemed to be waiting for this time with a special joy. Yet she had one last struggle to undergo. At one point, she seemed to see the devil, and cried in a loud voice: "Go away, go away, go away!" When peace returned, she said to her sisters: "Now it is near midnight, when Jesus was born and lay in the manger, and he created his new star with the greatest power, such as was never seen by anyone before." Her exultant joy seemed complete. Sometime after midnight, very early on November 17, 1231, she gave her soul to God.

They bound her face with cloth and carried her, dressed her in her gray tunic, to the hospital chapel. People came from all around Marburg and the surrounding areas to see her. They were amazed at the fragrant odor her body gave off, an odor that "refreshed the spirit." Carried away by devotion, they cut off pieces of her clothes for relics, along with her hair, bits of her flesh and even the tips of her breasts.

Elizabeth remained unburied for three days to give all the crowds a chance to see her; she was to be buried on Wednesday.

As vigils were being sung over her body, Lutrude the Abbess of the Augustinian monastery of Wetter, who was attending, heard birds singing nearby. When she went outside, she saw a great variety of birds sitting on the church spire and singing, each in its own way, Elizabeth's funeral rites.

The first miracle was reported at Elizabeth's tomb on the day after her burial: a Cistercian monk was healed of a mental affliction. When people heard of this, they began flocking in large numbers. Many took earth from her grave to put on blind eyes or afflicted limbs. The hospital chapel was soon too large to accommodate the vast number of pilgrims. Conrad of Marburg, who had been appointed protector of the hospital by the Pope, began to direct the building of a stone basilica with a long, slender nave around her grave. The crowds continued to increase. Caesarius of Heisterbach recalled: "I was there around that time and I do not recall ever in my whole life seeing so many people at once, as I saw in the town of Marburg and around it then. Only with the greatest difficulty could anyone get in or out of the church."[1]

In the meantime, Raymond of Peñafort, a Dominican, and the Pope's penitentiary, had begun asking Conrad for details of the miracles, which were already widely known outside of Germany. We tend to forget that Elizabeth's tomb was to her time what Lourdes is to ours. It was soon to become one of the greatest places of pilgrimage in the Catholic world.

On August 10, 1232, not yet nine months after Elizabeth's death, Archbishop Siegfried of Mainz came to dedicate two altars in the church. Conrad, who preached the sermon, invited anyone in the crowd who had experienced a miracle through her intercession to come again the next day to testify to it before the bishop and other prelates and abbots present. On August 11, testimony on 60 miracles was taken down, which, as Conrad pointed out to the Pope, were only "the more striking ones."

In their report, the prelates added that they had omitted many cases because "on account of the crowds of people, many of them could not be brought before us."[2] But the prelates did not only write down the testimony of others. Along with a vast multitude, assembled again for Master Conrad's preaching, they actually saw the cures of a seven-year-old blind boy and another boy crippled from birth take place before their eyes.

In his letter to the Pope accompanying the miracles, Conrad included a brief summary of Elizabeth's life and virtues as he knew them from personal experience. Given the fact that it normally took a month or longer for messengers to get from Germany to Rome, the Pope must have acted very quickly after receiving this packet of documents. By mandates of October 13 and 14, 1232, he appointed a commission, consisting of Archbishop Siegfried of Mainz, Abbot Raymond of Eberbach and Master Conrad of Marburg, to inquire into Elizabeth's virtues and miracles. They were asked to hold on to the results of this investigation until the arrival of another mandate directing that they be sent to Rome.

This investigation was held in January 1233, and took place, like the first, in the new basilica next to Elizabeth's hospital in Marburg. The number of people who had come to testify, as well as the crowd of onlookers, was so great that the people overflowed not only the church, but the town and the surrounding villages; many were forced to camp in the mountains and the woods; so great was the multitude that there was a severe food shortage in the area.

A total of 106 miracles were recorded at these hearings, along with testimonies on Elizabeth's life and virtues by her "religious and God-fearing household"[3] and others who knew her. No record of the depositions on her virtues has been preserved, but the vivid testimonies on the miracles still survive.

In one, a fifty-year-old woman named Matilda of Biedenkopf, of the diocese of Mainz, who had been blind in one eye, testified that as she was on her way to Elizabeth's tomb, "she heard people singing a German song about the separation of a tearful Elizabeth from her husband, the Landgraf Ludwig, as he was about to leave for the Holy Land. This song moved Matilda to tears; while she was weeping, she recovered the sight in her eye."[4] Troubadours and Minnesingers composed a number of such farewell songs during the period of the Crusades. In one, Count Otto of Botenlauben wrote: "if the reward of Christ were not so sweet, I would not leave my beloved lady whom I salute many times in my heart."[5] The song that the pilgrims sang on their journey to Elizabeth's tomb gives us a vivid picture of how people recalled her: she was not only a saint, but a courtly lady, and a loving wife. These things made her seem close to them. They recalled that she was a mother as well: a very large proportion of the miracles involved the healing of children.

The process now came to a standstill for a time. In part, the delay may have come about because of the controversy that broke out between Conrad of Marburg and fellow commission member Siegfried of Mainz. Conrad, who was appointed papal inquisitor shortly after Elizabeth's death, acted without restraint, sending many people accused of heresy to the stake without allowing them to speak on their own behalf or call witnesses in their defense. Siegfried opposed his over-zealous approach. Conrad even accused some of the high German nobility of heresy. The Pope had to intervene. Then, on July 30, 1233, Conrad was assassinated, apparently on the orders of some of the accused nobles. He was buried beside Elizabeth in her church in Marburg.

No further progress was made in Elizabeth's cause for about a year. But in the summer of 1234, her brother-in-law

Conrad visited Rome and spoke with the Pope about her process. He and his brother, the Landgraf Heinrich, had found Elizabeth a very inconvenient sister-in-law just a few years before, but now she would bring great renown to their house if she were declared a saint! Yet Conrad seems to have undergone a sincere religious conversion; he had joined the hospital order of the Teutonic Knights.

Gregory IX welcomed Conrad's visit, and on October 11, 1234, he sent a second set of mandates to Bishop Conrad of Hildesheim and the abbots of Georgenthal and Hersfeld, authorizing them to send the results of the previous investigation into Elizabeth's miracles to the Holy See, or if these were not available, to carry out a new investigation of trustworthy witnesses.

The new commission held a second set of hearings in January 1235. It is these from which the Statements of the Four Handmaids (known as the *Dicta*) are drawn. But because of the discovery of the Anonymous Franciscan, we now know that even more testimonies were taken down during the investigations of both 1233 and 1235 than are contained in the *Dicta*.

When the commissioners' final report had been prepared, a delegation was chosen to take it to the Pope: it consisted of Bernard, the abbot of Buch, Master Solomon, preacher of God's word, and Elizabeth's brother-in-law Conrad. A consistory was called in Perugia, where the papal court was staying at the time, and the report on Elizabeth's virtues and miracles was read before the Pope, the patriarchs of Antioch and Jerusalem, the College of Cardinals and many bishops and other assembled prelates. They gave their unanimous approval for Elizabeth's canonization.

On Pentecost Sunday, May 27, 1235, the Pope and assembled prelates, accompanied by an enormous crowd, went in procession to the jubilant sound of horns and trumpets, to the church and convent of St. Dominic in Perugia. There Landgraf

Conrad distributed large candles to the Pope, prelates and religious, and ordinary smaller candles to the multitude. The cardinal deacon, who assisted the Pope during ceremonies, read and expounded Elizabeth's life and miracles to the people. Then, to the singing of the "Gloria" and applause sweeping through the multitude, Elizabeth was solemnly declared a saint.

Afterwards, Conrad of Thuringia gave generous gifts of food to all the local convents, including the Franciscans. The Pope had Conrad sit beside him at dinner and gave him every sign of favor.[6]

In his bull of canonization, the Pope eloquently celebrated Elizabeth's love for the poor, and the way in which, by simply practicing the Gospel Beatitudes, she had already won many areas of Germany back from the heretics.

The Pope was eager to propose Elizabeth as an example to the whole Church. In fact, according to Caesarius of Heisterbach, "His devotion for her was so great that he sent special letters to the different religious orders of the Church, asking and ordering that they celebrate the feast day of St. Elizabeth, which they did."[7]

The elevation of Elizabeth's body in order to place it in a new shrine was to take place on May 1, 1236. The whole ruling family of Thuringia was to have a prominent place. The Emperor Frederick II himself was scheduled to come. Three days before the event, the brothers of the Teutonic Order, who had taken over the running of Elizabeth's hospital, opened her tomb, and found her body completely incorrupt, her arms crossed on her breast.

The day for the translation came. A huge crowd gathered from Germany, France, Bohemia and Hungary. The Emperor arrived and joined the procession in penitential garb. Elizabeth's head was removed and Frederick placed a golden crown on it before the multitude. Soon people noticed that a fragrant oil was flowing in abundance from the saint's body. It proved as powerful in healing the sick as the earth from her tomb had been in the years following her burial.

Elizabeth's children were also there that day. Hermann, the oldest, was fourteen. Beside him were twelve-year-old Sophia and nine-year-old Gertrude, accompanied no doubt by some nuns of the convent in Altenberg, where she lived as an oblate. This is the last time history records all three children standing together, so this is the best place to describe their future lives. Hermann II, Elizabeth's son, was the heir to his father's lands and titles. We learn very little about his early years. But his family had always had great hopes for him, perhaps even one day as Emperor to succeed Frederick II. Yet, according to the Anonymous Franciscan, Elizabeth told some of the friars in Marburg, "I would rather have my son a true Friar Minor than to have him King and Emperor of the whole world." She knew, of course, that such a religious vocation was most likely not his destiny. He would do great good in the world if he were a good ruler like his father. But she wanted her children to honor God and their souls above all things.

We do know that at the age of twelve, Hermann was old enough to be associated with his uncle Heinrich Raspe in the government of Thuringia. He was betrothed for the first time in 1238 to Margaret, the daughter of Frederick II and his third wife, Isabel of England, though Margaret was only a year old at the time. This close relationship with the Emperor's family was a sign of the great expectations for his future. But when Frederick, who had always been a thorn in the Pope's side, broke off relations with the papacy, Hermann chose to remain loyal to the Pope, and gave his support to Otto of Brunswick instead, marrying Otto's daughter Helen on October 9, 1239, at the age of seventeen. She was a more suitable age, just a year younger than he was.

In 1240, we find Hermann staying at the court of the saintly King Louis IX of France. He made a favorable impression on the king's seneschal, Sieur Jean de Joinville, who recalled him, during a magnificent feast given by Louis in Saumur in Anjou, waiting at table on the Queen mother, Blanche of Castile, along with two other young noblemen, the Count of Boulogne and the Count of St. Pol. This attitude of service was one very dear to his mother. He also made an impression on Queen Blanche, who "often kissed him on the forehead out of devotion, because she had heard that his mother had kissed him there many times."[8]

Hermann now began to rule with full power in Thuringia, but his young life full of promise was soon cut short. He died suddenly on January 3, 1241, when he was not yet nineteen, and was succeeded by his uncle, Heinrich Raspe. The *Chronicle of Reinhardsbrunn* hints that Hermann was poisoned by Bertha von Seebach, the wife of a noble at court; a conclusion that bystanders reached by noting that Hermann's corpse bled at the nostrils when Bertha was near; it was an old Germanic superstition that a corpse would bleed at the presence of the murderer. However, even the chronicler doesn't seem to believe this tale entirely. Later writers even throw suspicion on Heinrich Raspe as the murderer, plotting to take the throne, but the evidence for this is even less credible. Unfortunately, because of the lack of medical knowledge, only too many young people died of unknown illnesses in the Middle Ages before reaching full maturity, and this is most likely what happened to Hermann.

Elizabeth's second child, Sophia, married Henry the Duke of Brabant at the age of 17 in 1241, and they had a son named Heinrich. When Sophia's uncle Heinrich Raspe died childless in 1247, the original male line of the Landgraves of Thuringia came to an end. Sophia, who was as strong-willed as Elizabeth and her grandmother Gertrude of Hungary, fought and negotiated to have her young son continue the family line against Heinrich of Meissen and Hermann of Henneburg, the children of Ludwig's older sister, and Siegfried of Anhalt, son of Ludwig's sister Irmingard. She kept up her campaign for a great many years; eventually her son became Heinrich I, Landgraf of Hesse when the territory was separated from Thuringia. The house of Hesse was powerful and prolific; because of this, most of the remaining royalty in Europe is in one way or another descended from Elizabeth through this daughter. Sophia contributed greatly to the magnificent church built to honor her mother. She died in Marburg on May 29, 1275.

The youngest child, Gertrude, who was brought up at the Premonstratensian monastery of Altenberg, chose to follow her parents' wishes and became a nun there; she was elected abbess of the community at the age of twenty-one, and remained in office for almost 50 years, until her death. She built the monastery's beautiful Gothic church. She was known for saying, "the higher and more noble you are, the more you must humble yourself in all things." It is almost as if we were listening to Elizabeth herself.

Sophia kept in close contact with her sister, and may have introduced her to the Eucharist devotion in the Low Countries, especially the feast of the Blessed Sacrament, which Gertrude established at her monastery in 1270. The feast had been founded in 1246 in Liege by St. Julianna, also a Premonstratensian. Gertrude also followed the crusading tradition of her family: during the Seventh Crusade, she and her nuns "took the cross," praying and doing penance for its success. She also maintained her mother's devotion to the poor: she built a hospital near her monastery and like Elizabeth, nursed the sick there herself. She died in 1297 at the age of seventy, and her cult was confirmed in 1348 by Pope Clement VI; she is known as Blessed Gertrude of Altenberg.[9]

This daughter of St. Elizabeth was the crowning glory of a family which had already produced a number of saints. Ludwig too, was honored among the people of Thuringia for his holiness, though he was never canonized. The days of earthly glory in Thuringia did not long outlast Elizabeth and Ludwig's deaths; but the spiritual glory they brought is far more lasting,

XII. Elizabeth's Legacy

In the eight hundred years following Elizabeth's death, religious orders have taken their inspiration from her, hundreds of churches have been named for her, great Christian art has been dedicated to her, and charitable societies have been founded in her name. Many people all over the world have reason to be grateful to her and imitate her. But I would like to recall the things that make her a particularly vital saint for our time.

First, young people need a role model like her more than ever. In a world that seems to encourage an adolescent mentality in adults of 35 and 40, and where genuine adolescents are given more leisure, more money, more pleasures, but less responsibility and less reason to live than in any society in history, Elizabeth is proof that youth is not a barrier to accomplishing great things and becoming spiritually mature. In fact, she did more for God in her short life of twenty-four years than many people do in eighty.

By the age of eighteen or nineteen, she was not only already shouldering the responsibility of a family, but caring for the lives of the poor, building a hospital and making serious decisions in regard to the social system of a whole country.

Young people can learn from her that they too, can make a difference. Not only this, but they too can rely on a close relationship to God to help them accomplish any task they face in life.

Second, in Elizabeth we have a vital example of secular spirituality, the type of spirituality that lay people and those of us who are in secular orders follow. Secular means "in the world." Those who follow this way of life must reject worldliness, but not the world. A secular spirituality looks to building up a just world, and consecrating our actions in the world to God. Some Christians have kept themselves from any interest in the culture around them out of fear of contamination. To love the world in a proper way, however, to be really "secular," we must participate in the culture around us, without adopting all of its beliefs. As a ruler at one of Europe's most glittering courts, Elizabeth found many ways to use her position to serve God and others; she recognized all the dangers and temptations of this life, but used it nonetheless to try to create a more just society, and to bring the problems of the poor to the attention of the great. We can follow her example in our culture today, not matter what our position, wherever there is a need for charity and justice.

For those of us who are Secular Franciscans, Elizabeth is an example of the way to live the life of penance we are called to in the world. The marks of the Franciscan concept of penance are first, "continued conversion," by which we remove ourselves from the center of our being and place God there, and second, acts of compassion and charity toward our brothers and sisters, especially the poorest.[1] We try to build a more peaceful and fraternal world. Elizabeth followed the penitential life at court, placing God at the center of her life, and always striving to be closer to him. In her married life, she often wore garments of penance, and engaged in prayer. She dedicated her life to serving the poor. She eventually became a penitent, dedicating herself totally to God. Throughout her life, she sought to create a new ideal of fraternity that was not bound by social barriers, but that included everyone, rich and poor.

Third, Elizabeth is a very important example to all those today who struggle to protect human life in our "culture of death." In his bull of canonization, Pope Gregory IX wrote that the heretics were able to see "the vast regions of Germany which they have tried to poison by their doctrine of death exult in many ways in the embrace of heavenly doctrine."

"The doctrine of death"—how familiar those words seem today! In fact, the attack on human life in Elizabeth's day had origins similar to the one in ours. Above all, distorted views of human sexuality played a large role. In the thirteenth century, the Cathars saw reproductive sexuality as evil. This belief was echoed on the opposite side by the some of the ideas associated with courtly love as expressed in the poetry of the troubadours, which had taken root in Provence, one of the major centers of Cathar activity. Here the intention was anything but religious, but the result was the same. Love was often seen merely as a fulfilling of the physical desires of the lovers and was often thought best when it took place outside of marriage. Some of the courtly love texts, in fact, made reference to contraceptive practices.

Today's "culture of death" relies on the same distorted views of sexuality. Many people, soaked in sensuality but strangely despising nature, see the normal end of sexuality, the birth of a child, as a terrible tragedy, as did the Cathars. Many also see sex in the same way as the courtly writers did, as best when freed from marriage and children. Consequently they turn away from the care God asks us to have for each and every human life toward a teaching that their own convenience and pleasure must be preserved, even at the expense of the lives of others, especially the unborn and newborn; but it also extends to the handicapped, the weak, the aged, all those who are considered a "burden" to society. Elizabeth's example is the perfect answer to this poisonous doctrine, an answer she expressed in actions rather than words, in her unwavering care for the those lives that others neglected or despised.

During World War II, Father Alfred Delp, a courageous Jesuit priest, delivered a sermon for St. Elizabeth on her feast day, November 17, in the church of Sankt Georg in Bavaria. Knowing that a Nazi spy was listening in the church, he spoke, though in veiled terms, of the regime's medical experimentation on the mentally and physically handicapped, and the killing of those deemed unfit to live. But St. Elizabeth, he said, teaches us "the true meaning of human life":

> Those who gathered around Elizabeth were not men with ringing steps; they were not men with blazing eyes and ramrod posture; they were not men of high rank. No, they were the cripples, the chronically ill, the retarded, the poor and every kind of outcast from normal life and existence—from the highways and hedgerows, from the asylums— the lost and the helpless . . . Alas, what was the purpose of those stunted lives? Ordinarily, no one would find any joy in them. But whoever has eyes to see what the Lord God intends for mankind recognizes that even in the most despised and derelict of human beings there is something that we are obliged to revere, that we must aid, that we must guard and nurture; the face of the Lord God Himself, who said, "I have formed man in my own image and likeness." And who may take it upon himself to annihilate this image and likeness, formed by the intelligence, will and love of God? This quiet woman bears a grave and urgent message for our land, for our people, for each of us: everywhere,

wherever we find ourselves, wherever we may be called upon to bear witness, we must protect life, we must guard human beings from everything that can crush them underfoot. Woe to those who inflict suffering! And woe to those who have destroyed a human life, who have desecrated an image of God, even when it was already breathing its last, even when it seemed to represent only a vestige of humanity.[2]

The example of St. Elizabeth, who saw the image of God in every single human being, is more important than ever today, when we are living in a society that finds the elderly, the dying and handicapped inconveniences, and when the holocaust of abortion has already taken so many innocent lives—many times more than perished in the Nazi death camps. But of all the legacies Elizabeth has left us, perhaps the greatest is her example of how we are to love each other and God.

Elizabeth loved everyone she was given by God to love, and did it whole-heartedly. We need never fear loving our loved ones too much. We are unlikely to ever have enough love in us to give everything to others that they need. Nor should we worry about our love being "too earthly" rather than "heavenly" as long as its end is directed to God and submitted to his will. It is those earthly things that are destined to lead most of us to heaven. Elizabeth her loved husband and children as a way to God. But circumstances and God's will may make it necessary for us to sacrifice everything for God as Elizabeth did. She once said, perhaps thinking of people like Master Conrad, that those who wept and did penance with gloomy faces "seem almost to frighten the Lord; let them give to God what they have with joy and cheerfulness." She lost her beloved husband, her home, and finally her children, but was able to give them to God cheerfully out of love for him, her greatest good. She had found the center and secret of human life. For as St. Paul said: "So faith, hope and love remain, these three; but the greatest of these is love" (1 Cor. 13:13).

Let us all pray that we might love God and our neighbor as Elizabeth did.

Appendix: The Expulsion

"After her husband's death, Elizabeth was ejected from the castle and all the possessions of her dower by some of her husband's vassals, since her husband's brother was still young." These words of Isentrude have provoked bitter controversy for over a hundred years among scholars studying Elizabeth's life. That she was physically expelled from a castle was regarded as simple fact by her medieval biographers, and repeated for centuries in lives of her. Later legends actually declared that it was Elizabeth's brothers-in-law, Heinrich and Conrad, and even her mother-in-law Sophia, who expelled her from the Wartburg—something none of the early sources say.

In the late nineteenth and twentieth centuries, some scholars, including Karl Wenck, Jean Ancelet-Hustache and many of Elizabeth's popular biographers, rejected the traditional interpretation. For them, the words "expelled by some of her husband's vassals" should be interpreted thus: the officials were following the orders of the Landgraf's family to deny Elizabeth the free use of her dower property, which she depended on to be able to provide for herself and her retinue and avoid eating food that had been unlawfully acquired. They believe, in fact, that Isentrude's statement simply means that Elizabeth voluntarily left her life at Wartburg castle as a result of this change, in order to be able to obey her conscience in regard to food, and to live the life of Franciscan poverty. For this view, they rely entirely on the deposition of Irmingard, who says:

"After her husband died, Blessed Elizabeth was temporarily not allowed to use her husband's property, because she was prevented from doing so by her husband's brother. She could have received some sustenance from her husband's brother, but she did not want to receive her nourishment by theft and by taxing the poor, as was so often the practice at the courts of princes. She chose to be abject and to earn her bread by the work of her hands like a day laborer." Irmingard's statement is important as a summary of the whole of this period of Elizabeth's life and the ultimate choice she made (in fact, it probably refers to the time when, as Dietrich of Apolda recounts, she was invited to return to the Wartburg by her brothers-in-law until the matter of her property could be resolved).

But Irmingard was not an eyewitness to these events. Strangely, almost no one has taken seriously the direct statement by Isentrude, an eyewitness, that *Elizabeth was expelled from her dower castle by some of her husband's vassals.* In trying to discover what really happened, we are faced with the strange silence of our main sources on some points. Isentrude never names either the castle from which Elizabeth was expelled, or the town below it in which she took refuge. Nor does she give the names or positions of the vassals. Nor does any other early source: neither the *Libellus*, nor the life by Caesarius of Heisterbach, nor even Dietrich of Apolda, for all his dependence on local Thuringian tradition. Mention of the Wartburg appears only in the fourteenth-century *Chronicle of Reinhardsbrunn*, and the lives and traditions on Elizabeth from the fifteenth-century onward. Most of Elizabeth's modern biographers have reacted strongly against the later stories about her being personally expelled by her in-laws, because of their lack of foundation. But they have gone to an extreme in the opposite direction and have believed that Isentrude's words cannot have meant a physical expulsion at all.

Historian Albert Huyskens, who studied the question carefully back in 1908, did take Isentrude's words seriously, and wrote what I believe is the best treatment of the subject. He pointed out that if the expulsion is to be seen as taking place from Elizabeth's dower castle, as Isentrude's words clearly imply, this castle certainly could not have been the Wartburg, for it was totally against the custom of the nobility to give the family's main castle to a wife as a dower. And in fact, one of our very earliest sources, the *Libellus,* names the town of Marburg, including the castle overlooking the city, as Elizabeth's dower property. Therefore, he said, Elizabeth must have been expelled from her properties and castle in Marburg.[1]

It is very hard to dispute Huyskens' logical conclusion, though critics have almost completely overlooked his argument. In focusing on the single sentence in Isentrude's testimony quoted above, scholars have ignored the fact that she speaks clearly about an expulsion in the physical sense not just in one place, but in several: she stresses that Elizabeth had nowhere to go, that no one dared give her shelter, that she was even confined against her will. There is no doubt that Isentrude is talking about an actual physical expulsion that sent Elizabeth into hiding, and a persecution that apparently extended to anyone who might have tried to help her. The whole atmosphere of her narration is one of force and fear of violence. To reject the physical expulsion would mean rejecting the whole of Isentrude's testimony about this period of Elizabeth's life.

And yet this is what some of Elizabeth's biographers have done. Their attempts to harmonize the details of this account with their hypothesis of a voluntary abandonment of her previous life are all very unconvincing. Ancelet-Hustache herself admitted that there is no good explanation as to why Elizabeth, if she left the Wartburg voluntarily, could not have gone to stay with her mother-in-law Sophia and the Cistercian nuns at St. Katherine's in Eisenach, or why, if she left voluntarily, people "did not dare" to give her shelter and she was forced to stay with enemies who treated her badly.

Some have objected that the woman who pushed her into the mud, mentioned by Isentrude, had earlier received alms from her, so this incident must have taken place in Eisenach, where Elizabeth spent most of her life. But Elizabeth had previously administered her lands in Marburg, and had most likely visited them and given charity to the people there. Some have objected that she received the land in Marburg on which she built her hospital from her brothers-in-law as compensation for her dower, not from her husband. In fact, a letter by Heinrich and Conrad does indicate that they gave her the land. But since they were indemnifying her for her dower, it would have been perfectly natural for them to have given her a piece of the same dower land she had before, which the *Libellus* explicitly states that she received from her husband.

Women of the ruling class in the Middle Ages frequently played a part in dynastic power struggles, and Elizabeth may have suffered from her enemies the effects of her own stand for justice, which was in the end, political as well as religious. For her to undergo actual physical expulsion and imprisonment would not have been out of the ordinary. Ancelet-Hustache believed that Elizabeth "knew nothing about politics,"[2] but this is very unlikely, given her position and her obvious intelligence. In a world where the Landgraf Ludwig could go to war against his own sister, what happened to Elizabeth does not seem so unusual.

Isentrude's lack of clarity about details is not surprising. After all, the powerful ruling family of Thuringia, in the person of Elizabeth's brother-in-law Conrad, was by now, in 1235, directing her canonization process. And, if the hints Isentrude gives are accurate, Conrad and his brother Heinrich were at least indirectly responsible for Elizabeth's sufferings, and may have acted in complicity with those who forced her out of her home. Isentrude, a noblewoman, may have been unwilling to say anything against Heinrich, the brother she spoke about, especially since, as a long-time member of the Landgraf's household, she had probably known him well personally and did not want to accuse him directly, especially without proof. She had to be discreet—but her words are clear enough that there can be no doubt about at least the outlines of what happened, although it is necessary to speculate in order to fill in the details.[3]

Part II

In the Words of Those

Who Knew Her

Letter by Conrad of Marburg

Shortly after August 11, 1232

Your Holiness, Reverend Father,

As you must know, your penitentiary, Brother Raymond,[1] has written to me several times, asking me to certify for you the miracles that God has worked through Lady Elizabeth, the late Landgrafin of Thuringia, whom Your Paternity had commended to me so that I might serve as her procurator.

Therefore recently, on the feast day of St. Lawrence,[2] the Lord Archbishop of Mainz—not only because of my petition, but also because he evidently received it in a revelation—dedicated two altars in the basilica where the body of the said lady is buried. On that day I also called a great multitude of people to that place, for the preaching as well as the dedication.

During the course of the sermon, without any consultation at all beforehand, conceiving in my mind the desire to satisfy Your Holiness about the certification of the miracles, I ordered all those present who had received cures through the merit of the Landgrafin to present themselves around the first hour of the following day, with any witnesses they might have, before my Lord of Mainz and the other prelates who had gathered for the dedication, to have it faithfully confirmed that they had received grace by invoking her.

So a quite large crowd, all of whom claimed to have received cures from her, gathered together. My Lord of Mainz, because he was in a hurry to attend to some other urgent business, wrote down the more important evidence and had it confirmed with his seal, as well as those of the other prelates. The testimonies taken by several of the prelates and important men who were there have been omitted, for they did not have their seals with them. And now, so that you might be more fully informed not only about [Elizabeth's] miracles, but also about the way she lived, I am writing down for you a summary of her life.

For two years before she was commended to me, while her husband was alive, I was her confessor. I found her lamenting that she had ever been joined in marriage, and that she had not been able to end her life in the flower of her virginity. At the time that her husband set out to join the emperor in Apulia, so severe a famine arose throughout all of Germany that many people were dying of hunger. Now Sister Elizabeth began to grow strong in virtue. Just as throughout her life she was the consoler of the poor, she now fully became the restorer of the starving. She ordered a hospital to be built for her next to a certain castle of hers, in which she gathered a number of sick and weak people. She distributed in abundance the benefits of charity to everyone who asked her for alms there, and not only there, but to all the borders and limits of her husband's jurisdiction. In this way, she gave away all of the crop from her husband's four principalities. She even sold all her jewelry and expensive clothes for the use of the poor. It was her habit to personally visit all of her sick twice a day, morning and evening, and to nurse those that were more abhorrent than the others herself. She fed them, smoothed their beds, lifted them on her shoulders, and performed many other services of humanity. And all these things were found not to be against the will of her husband of happy memory.

At length, after her husband's death, when Your Holiness saw fit to recommend her to me, in her desire to attain the highest perfection, she consulted me as to whether she could acquire more merit as a recluse, or in a cloister, or in some other state. Finally she had an idea firmly in mind, which with many tears, she begged me to grant her, namely, to permit her to beg from door to door.

When I vehemently refused this, she answered: "I will do this, for you can't forbid me." And on Good Friday, when the altars were stripped, she placed her hands on the altar in one of the chapels of her city where she had established the Friars Minor. There, in the presence of some of the brothers, her relatives and her children,[3] she renounced her own will, all the pomp of the world, and everything that the Savior of the world counsels us to forsake in his Gospel. And when she wanted to renounce her possessions, I prevented her, partly so that she might repay her husband's debts, and partly on account of the needy, for I was minded to have her aid them with those things which belonged to her through her dower. When this was done, she saw that she might be absorbed by the tumult and glory of the world, on those lands on which she had lived so gloriously when her husband was alive. So, although I was unwilling, she followed me to Marburg, which was at the farthest boundaries of her husband's lands.

There in the town she built a hospital, and gathered the sick and feeble in it. She placed the most wretched and despised next to her at her table. When I criticized her for this, she answered that she received a singular grace and humility from them. Like an undoubtedly prudent woman, recalling to me her past life, she said that it was necessary for her in this way to treat contraries by contraries.[4] When I saw that she wanted to make [spiritual] progress, I cut her off from all unnecessary members of her household, and ordered her to be content with three people:

a lay brother who carried out her business affairs, a religious virgin of very low birth, and a noble widow, who was deaf and very severe. This was so that through the handmaid her humility might be increased, and through the severe widow she might be stimulated to patience. In fact, while the handmaid prepared vegetables, the lady washed dishes, and vice versa.

Among other things, she took in a paralyzed orphan boy who was suffering from a constant flow of blood[5] and placed him at night in her bed for the greater exercise [of charity]. She suffered many afflictions because of him, for sometimes six times a night, sometimes more, she would carry him in her arms for the call of nature, and with her own hands she would wash his soiled clothes, as is usually done in such cases. When he was dead, she took in a leper girl to care for, without my knowledge, and hid her in her home, taking on herself all the services of humanity. She humbled herself, not only by feeding her and making her bed and washing her, but also by taking off her shoes, especially begging the members of her household not to be offended by these things. When I became aware of this, because I was afraid that she would be infected by the disease—may God forgive me!—I punished her very severely.

Finally, after I had thrown the leper girl out, and I had withdrawn to remote areas to carry out my preaching work, she undertook to cure a poor little boy who was so completely full of scabies that he did not have a single hair on his head.[6] By both washing him and giving him medication—where she learned it, I don't know—she cured him. This boy was seated by her bed as she lay dying.

In spite of these works of the active life, I declare before God that I have rarely seen a more contemplative woman. For some men and women religious frequently saw her as she was coming from her secret prayers, with her face wondrously radiant, as though sunbeams were coming from her eyes. Indeed, very often when she was sent into ecstasy of soul, for a very long time afterwards, she would take very little or no nourishment from food.

Finally the time of her death drew near, yet she was still healthy. Since I was tormented at that time by a very serious illness, I asked her how she wanted to arrange her way of life when I was dead. When I asked that question, she predicted her own death to me without hesitation. In fact, on the fourth day after this conversation, she fell into an illness from which she suffered for more than twelve days. Three days before her death, she had all lay people excluded from her. She did not even permit the nobles who frequently came to visit her to enter. When they complained and asked why they were thus excluded from sitting around her bed, she said that she wanted to meditate on her end, the severity of her judgment and her omnipotent judge.

Afterwards on Sunday, which was the one before the octave of St. Martin [November 16, 1231], I heard her confession after Matins were sung, but she recalled nothing at all that she had not confessed to me several times. When I asked her what should be done with her belongings and household goods, she answered that everything that up till then seemed to be hers belonged to the poor, and asked me to distribute everything of hers except a poor habit in which she was dressed, and in which she wanted to be buried.

When these things were done, about the first hour, she received the body of the Lord. Afterwards, up until the hour of vespers, she frequently spoke about the excellent things she had heard in sermons, and most of all about the raising of Lazarus and how the Lord wept over his raising. And when these words made some men and women religious weep, she said, "Daughters of Jerusalem, weep not for me, but for yourselves."[7] After she said this, she was silent, and though her lips did not move, sweet voices were heard in her throat. And when those who were sitting around asked her what it was, she asked them if they did not hear with her some people singing. After this at sunset she lay back as though exulting and showing signs of devotion, until the first cockcrow. And then she said: "Behold, the hour when the Virgin gave birth." Then, devoutly commending all those sitting near her to God, as though gently falling asleep, she died.

On learning of her death, the monks of the Cistercian Order and many other religious came together from all sides to the hospital where she was to be buried. The devotion of the people made it necessary for her to remain unburied until the following Wednesday. She had absolutely no sign of death about her except that she had grown pale, for her body remained as soft as though she were alive and gave off a very pleasant fragrance. The day after her burial, the Lord immediately began to work through his handmaid, for a monk of the Cistercian Order was cured at her tomb of a mental illness from which he had suffered for more than forty years. He swore to this before me and the parish priest of Marburg.

She died on November 16, at the age of twenty-four.[8]

Statements of the Four Handmaids of St. Elizabeth

January 1235

Guda, a virgin in religious life, who was attached to blessed Elizabeth from the time that she was around five years old and Elizabeth was four, was asked about her life and the way she conducted herself. She stated under oath that blessed Elizabeth, the late Landgrafin of Thuringia, the daughter of the king of Hungary, was devoted to religion from her youth. She directed all her desires and actions to God, in her games as well as in serious matters.

For when she was five years old and did not know how to read at all, she frequently prostrated herself in front of the altar, opening the psalter in front of her as if she were praying. As a foreshadowing of her good character, she frequently performed genuflections in secret. She would cleverly find an opportunity to enter the chapel in a number of ways. For example, she was seen by her handmaids running toward the chapel, under the appearance of a game, as though trying to race some girl, and immediately on jumping in, she would pray intently in front of the altar, with her knees bent and with joined hands, with her lips pressed to the floor. Also, she would run away from the girls towards the chapel, hopping on one foot, as they did in one of their games. If she could not enter the chapel under this pretense of a game, she would hop over the threshold, and kiss the walls of the church.

In the ring game and any other game, she would place her hope of winning and getting a prize in God, and so that she would win, she would promise God several genuflections with Hail Marys. If she could not fulfill this promise, she would say slyly to some other little girl: "Let's measure which one of us is taller." And so she was able to make several genuflections while kneeling to measure her, as she herself often recalled afterwards as an adult.

In the ring game and other games, she would give a tenth part of her winnings to girls playing with her who were poorer than she was. She would give them little gifts, and for each gift she would obligate the recipient to say several Our Fathers and Hail Marys.

When she was a little older, for a long time she strove to obtain John the Evangelist, as the guardian of chastity, for her apostle. As was the custom among women, after placing all the apostles' names, each written either on a candle or on a piece of paper, mixed together on the altar, each one would draw an apostle for herself. After Elizabeth had prayed for what she wished, she received St. John as her apostle three times in the drawing of names.

She never refused anything that was asked in his honor, either a favor, or pardoning an offense or doing or giving up anything, whatever it might be. Also, when she was compelled to go to sleep without having completed her promised prayers, she frequently said them in bed.

Every day she deprived herself of something, breaking her will in something for the love of God. For instance, when she won anything in a game, she would say: "Now that I have won, I will stop for the love of God."

When several girls were dancing in a ring, after completing one round, she said to the others: "One is enough for me. I will give up the others for the love of God." And she did many other things like this.

She also used to make many small promises to God. For instance, she promised not to sew on her sleeves before Mass on feast days and not to use gloves on Sunday before noon. She abstained from these and other similar things pertaining to the adorning of the body and the vanities of the world, things that would take a long time to tell, because of her promise, out of reverence for God. She directed all things toward God in her adolescence too, keeping him humbly before her eyes, pronouncing his name sweetly, and invoking him in all her actions.

Much might be said about these matters; but because Guda does not recall any more at present, these few things must be enough.

When Guda was asked how long she remained with her and how she knew these things, she answered, as was said at the beginning above, that she was with Elizabeth serving her, and [remained with her] after the death of her lord the Landgraf until Blessed Elizabeth was professed, putting on the gray habit from the hand of Master Conrad. And at that time Guda herself put on the gray tunic with her, solemnizing with the habit the vow of chastity which she had made into Master Conrad's hands several years previously.

Isentrude, a religious of Horselgau, was in Blessed Elizabeth's household for around five years while her husband the Landgraf was alive, and remained with her for more than a year after his death until blessed Elizabeth put on the gray habit. She was so intimate with her that she knew all her secrets.

When she was put under oath and asked about Elizabeth's life, she stated that she always saw her, even when her husband was alive, to be devout, humble, very charitable, and very devoted to prayer. By walking quickly, she frequently arrived at church before the women in her retinue (who murmured and complained about it), so she could secretly perform a few genuflections.

While she was still in the proud dress of the world, she secretly took in a sick beggar, horrible in appearance, who was suffering from a scalp condition. She laid his head in her lap, and cut his shaggy hair with her own hands. Afterwards she washed his head in the privacy of her apple orchard, not wanting anyone to see her. When her handmaids surprised her at this and reproved her for it, she laughed about it.

Isentrude also said that while Blessed Elizabeth's husband was still alive, and with his consent, she made a vow of obedience to Master Conrad of Marburg, but with an exception for her husband's rights, and promised with her hands in Conrad's that she would preserve perpetual continence if she happened to survive her husband's death. This took place in Eisenach, in St. Katherine's monastery.

She also said that after Elizabeth had promised obedience to him, Master Conrad directed her not to make use of any of her husband's goods about which she did not have a clear conscience. She observed this so strictly that while sitting beside her husband at table, she abstained from everything that came from offices and the profits taken by officials, not using foods unless she knew that they came from her husband's own revenues and his legitimate possessions. When requisitioned goods were served, she often pretended to eat bread and other foods in front of the knights and servants, breaking them up and pushing them here and there, so it would look as if she were eating.

When she and three of the women of her retinue, who agreed to do this with her, asked the Landgraf not to be offended because they did not eat with the others, but pretended, he answered: "I would gladly do the very same thing, if I did not fear insults from the family and from others. Nevertheless, God willing, I will soon arrange my state of life differently."

Blessed Elizabeth provided for herself and her retinue out of some property especially assigned to her by the family as her dower. When nothing could be found for sale, she sent messengers to ask the more well-to-do people who lived near where she was staying at the time for what was necessary, as though she found those things more to her liking than the foods at court. But her real intention was to observe Master Conrad's orders. Conrad even prevented her from using any other goods at all which violated her conscience. So it often happened that she suffered from having nothing to eat. At times she ate nothing but some little cakes flavored with honey. And she and her servants were happily content with bread alone, if she had any which she could safely eat, because she was tormented by hunger and thirst amid the various courses served at her husband's table. Her husband always secretly reassured her about the foods that would be served.

One time, when she was eating with her husband, and abstaining from many sumptuous dishes that were profane, she had only five very small little birds, which had been sent to her. She kept part of them for herself, and sent the rest to her handmaids; she was content with these alone for dinner. She was actually afflicted more by her handmaids' want than by her own when she could not serve them legitimate goods. And so frequently, when she made inquiries of the servants of the estate managers, and found even a little licit food, she would say to her handmaids: "You are going to eat only." And when she found a little licit drink, perhaps from her husband's vineyards, she would say, "You are going to drink only."

When she knew both to be licit, she would clap her hands merrily and say, "Good for us, now we are going to eat and drink." It also happened that once, when she as to follow her husband to an important Diet, where he had already gone, she could not find any food which she dared use in conscience, except a little coarse, hard black bread, which she simply softened in hot water and ate. She and her retinue were content with this for dinner, because they fasted on Saturdays. And so they rode on horseback that same day eight German miles, which is fully equivalent to 40 Italian miles.[1]

Because of this singular and unusual way of life, both she and her husband, who permitted this, bore with great patience many insults from their people, even to their face. Even though she abstained from illicit procurements, wherever she could, she acquired, step by step, the ability to get enough to eat.

Blessed Elizabeth also rose frequently at night to pray, while her husband begged her not to afflict herself. And at times he held one of her hands in his as long as she prayed, begging her to get back in bed, concerned about her discomfort. So blessed Elizabeth frequently asked her ladies-in-waiting to awaken her at night for prayer, because she used to get up every night while her husband was sleeping—though sometimes he was only pretending to. Fearing to disturb her lord in waking her, they asked her how they should wake her. She instructed them to pull her by the foot.

Once Isentrude, in trying to wake her, pulled the lord by the foot, for he had thrown his leg over on his lady's side of the bed. He woke up, and knowing her intention, bore it patiently. Because of the length of her prayers, Elizabeth often fell asleep on the carpet in front of the bed. When her handmaids found fault with her for this, [and asked] why she would not rather sleep with her husband, she answered: "Although I cannot always pray, I can do violence to my flesh by tearing myself away from my beloved husband."

Also, rising from her husband's side, she would have herself severely scourged by the hands of her handmaids in a separate room, and after prayer she would return happily to her bed. She did this frequently after she promised obedience to Master Conrad. Previously, however, she had at times done the same thing in Lent and on Fridays. But when her husband was absent, she spent many nights in vigils, genuflections, scourging and prayers.

She also spoke about God with worldly matrons who came to see her, as though preaching to them. By urgently pleading with them, she frequently induced them to take a vow obliging them to abstain from at least one thing tending toward the vanity of the world, that is, if she could not persuade them to avoid several of these things: for instance, dances and too tightly-sewn sleeves, or silk ribbons for decorating their braided hair, and hairpins and other superfluous things. She wanted them to put on decent sleeves, suitable for good morals. Later, she would induce them to vow continence after their husbands' deaths.

Elizabeth was also in the habit, from her adolescence on, of very often unfastening her sleeves and removing the necklaces, rings, and other jewels from her body at [the reading of] certain Gospels, and to lay aside the veil adorning her head, before the time of the Gospel and the canon of the Mass. Similarly, she customarily assumed a humble and lowly posture, especially at the time when the Host was raised.

For the purification after the birth of each of her children when the customary number of days had passed, when other matrons were accustomed to come to the church in great pomp, with a large retinue and dressed in expensive clothes, she would come privately to the church, dressed in wool and barefoot, carrying her child in her own arms. She would offer her child on the altar, along with a candle and a lamb, after the example of the Blessed Virgin. Immediately on returning home, she would give the tunic and the cloak she had worn to a poor woman. On Rogation Days she would follow the procession of the cross dressed in wool and barefoot, and during the preaching at the stations she always chose a place among the poorest women.

While her husband was alive, Elizabeth would also spin wool with her maids, making it into cloth for the habits of the Friars Minor and clothes for the poor. She sewed garments with her own hands for poor catechumens. She would have them baptized, and would lift them from the sacred font, so that by becoming godmother to them she might more gladly benefit them. When a poor person who had died was to be buried, she would make his shroud with her own hands. She would handle and touch the dead with her own hands, and attended their funerals. She also cut a large, pure white linen sheet in pieces to wrap several dead people for burial. When she was visiting a poor man who was ill, and heard his complaint about some of his debts that he could not pay, she paid them for him.

She could not bear that the bodies of the rich should be wrapped in new linen or shirts, but [preferred them to be buried in] old ones, ordering that it was better to give those clothes to the poor. She frequently visited and consoled poor women in childbirth.

When messengers from these women or other sick people asked for anything from her, she would ask where they lived, so that by examining them, she would be inspired to mercy and compassion. No matter how distant their poor dwellings and no matter how muddy or difficult the road was, she would visit them, entering their shabby little rooms. She did not abhor their dirtiness; she brought them what was necessary, and consoled them, striving for a triple reward: from work, compassion, and generous giving. One day in a solitary place, she wanted to milk a cow so that she might satisfy the appetite of a poor person who was asking for milk, but the cow, behaving disrespectfully, would not stand for it.

Also, while her husband was alive, she was so obedient to Master Conrad that once when he called her to a sermon, and on account of the arrival of the Markgrafin of Meissen,[2] she could not come, Master Conrad was offended. He informed her through a messenger that from then on, he did not want to have charge of her because of this disobedience. The next day, she came with great haste and humbly begged him to forgive the offense. When he proved unwilling, she and her maids fell at his feet. Master Conrad imposed a penance on them: stripped to their undergarments, they were severely scourged by him.

At a time of general famine and want, when the Landgraf had gone to the court of Cremona, Elizabeth gave out the whole year's crop from his private granaries to the poor as alms. Every day she would give many people enough of what was necessary to sustain them. Below the very high castle where she was then living, there was a large building in which she placed many sick people who could not wait for the general alms. In spite of the great difficulty of going up and down, she visited them several times each day, consoling them and talking to them about patience and the salvation of the soul, and she satisfied the desire of each one in everything, even selling her jewels for their food.

And although she could not stand any corruption in the air anywhere else, she bore the corruption of the sick without any horror, even in summer, while her maids could scarcely stand it, finding it disagreeable and murmuring about it. She would cheerfully handle the sick with her own hands, and with the veil from her head she would wipe their faces, cleaning the saliva, sputum and filth from their mouths and nostrils. In addition to this, in the same house there were many poor children, for whom she provided well. She was so kind and gentle to them that they all called her "Mother." When she entered the house, they would all run to her and gather around her. Among them she especially loved those with scabies, the sick, the weak, and those who were the most dirty and deformed; she would take their heads with her hands and place them on her breast.

She gave the children little jars, glass rings and other play jewelry to console them. Once as she was riding from the town up to the castle, carrying all these things in her cloak, they accidentally fell from a very high, steep cliff and were dashed onto the stones. Although they fell on the rock, they were all found whole and safe, and afterwards she distributed them to the children to console them.

Also in addition to those sick people who shared in the common almsgiving to all the poor, she chose the poorer and weaker, whom she placed in front of the castle. She distributed to them what was left over from her table with her own hands, taking away much from herself and her handmaids in order to give it to the poor. One day after the giving of alms, when she distributed to them a small amount of beer remaining in a jar, and gave some to everyone, there was almost no lowering of the level in the tankard, but there remained as much as there was before.

And so she fed the multitude in this way until the new crop of grain came in. Then she gave smocks and shoes to all those who could work, so their feet would not be hurt by the stubble. She also gave them scythes, so they could gather in the harvest, and feed themselves by their own labor. To others who were truly weak and unable to work, she gave lightweight clothes, which she had distributed in the marketplace. She distributed all these things joyfully with her own hands, and when she dismissed the poor, she gave each one something. And when she did not have money, she gave poor little women expensive robes and other fine things of silk, saying to them: "I don't want you to use them for pleasure, but to sell them for your needs and work hard." She gave one of those women shoes, an undergarment and a surcote. The woman was so exhilarated that she fell to the ground, and was thought to be dying, crying out that never was there a greater joy in the world. When Blessed Elizabeth saw this, she was very upset, fearing that she would be the cause of her death.

Also, when she was at the height of her glory, she was greatly inclined to begging and frequently talked about poverty with her handmaids. And dressing herself before them in the palace in a shabby cloak and wrapping a plain piece of cloth around her head, she would say, "This is how I will walk when I go begging and bear misery for the love of God."

On Holy Thursday, she always solemnly performed the washing of the feet of the poor. On one Holy Thursday she gathered together many lepers, and prostrating herself most humbly at their feet, she washed their feet and hands, and kissed the most ulcerous and horrible places. And afterwards, wherever she found lepers, she sat next to them, consoling them and exhorting them to patience. She did not shrink from them more than from healthy people, and gave them very generous alms. She also avoided superfluous garments, abstaining completely from all long and costly gowns.

She exercised all her works of charity with constancy, and with the greatest cheerfulness of mind and face, while in secret she had the most fruitful grace of tears, which, however, poured joyfully down her face without deforming it. Elizabeth did all these and many other things worthy of recall, (which however, they [the witnesses] do not remember), during the lifetime of her husband, with whom she lived in marriage in a way worthy of praise. They loved each other with a wonderful affection, gently encouraging and strengthening each other in the praise and service of God. In fact, because her husband's attention was by necessity directed to the temporal needs of his principality —although in private he always had the fear of God before his eyes—he freely granted Blessed Elizabeth the authority to carry out all those things that pertained to the work and the honor of God, and promoting the salvation of souls.

The above-mentioned Guda agreed under oath with all these statements of Isentrude, because she was also at the same time in the household of Blessed Elizabeth.

After her husband's death, Elizabeth was ejected from the castle and all the possessions of her dower by some of her husband's vassals, since her husband's brother was still young. So she went into the town located below the castle, and entered a poor building in a courtyard belonging to an innkeeper, where he kept his dishes and household goods, and in which his pigs lay, and spent that night there in great joy. In the middle of the night, when it was time for Matins, she went to the Friars Minor in that town, asking them to sing the *Te Deum laudamus*, rejoicing and giving thanks to God for her tribulation.

The following day, when no rich man dared to offer her shelter, she entered the church together with her handmaids, and sat there a long time. And since her little ones had been brought from the castle in the most bitter cold, she did not know where she was to stay and where she was to lay her children's heads – although the lordship of the town belonged to them by succession to their father. Finally, compelled by necessity, she entered the home of a priest, asking him to have pity on her and her expelled children.

Afterwards, she was ordered to enter the home of one of her enemies, where she was forced to take refuge in a confined place with her whole household, although there were many buildings there. Because the host and hostess were very unpleasant to her and her retinue, on leaving there, she said farewell to the walls which had preserved her from the cold and rain, saying, "I would gladly thank the people, but I don't know why." And she returned again to the same dirty building where she had been at the beginning, because she was unable to get any other shelter.

And so, undergoing persecution from all her husband's men without cause and deprived of her property, she was forced by her poverty to send her children to different remote places, so that they might be brought up there. And she took the very little that she had out of her own mouth and spent on the poor. And a poor sick old woman, who had frequently received alms from her and money, as befitted her illnesses, met blessed Elizabeth going to church in a narrow street in a quarter of town where stones had been placed for crossing a deep mud puddle. The poor old woman, not wanting to make way, pushed Blessed Elizabeth in the mud, so that falling with all her clothes on, she became all dirtied. Bearing it patiently, laughing heartily, she got up and with joy washed her clothes.

While kneeling [in church] one day in Lent, she leaned against the wall for a very long time, with her eyes fastened on the altar. At last, when she returned to her humble dwelling and ate a small amount of food, because she was very weak, she began to sweat, and had to lean against the wall, until Isentrude caught her in her arms. And so after everyone except the said handmaid was sent from the room, [Elizabeth] had her eyes open, looking fixedly towards the window. At length, she began to laugh gently with great joy on her face. After a long time, her eyes closed, she shed countless tears, and a short time afterward she opened her eyes, laughing again very merrily as before. She lay in that contemplation until Compline, at times weeping with closed eyes and for a short time, and at times laughing with open eyes, but much more remaining in joy. At last, when she had been silent a long time, she suddenly burst forth with these words: "So then,

Lord, you want to be with me and I want to be with you and I never want to be separated from you."

Then Isentrude, a noblewoman who was more intimate with her than the rest of her ladies-in-waiting, asked her insistently to reveal to her with whom she had been speaking. Blessed Elizabeth, coming back to herself with difficulty, and finally overcome by her entreaties, answered: "I saw the heavens open and sweet Jesus my Lord bending down towards me and consoling me for the many difficulties and tribulations which surrounded me, and when I saw him, I was filled with joy and I laughed. But when he turned his face away, as if he were about to withdraw, I wept. Taking pity on me, he again turned his most serene face toward me, saying, 'If you want to be with me, I want to be with you,' to which I answered" [etc.]. Then Isentrude urged her to reveal the vision she saw in church when the host was offered, as was said above. To which Blessed Elizabeth answered: "It is better not to reveal what I saw there, but you should know that I was in the greatest joy, and I saw wonderful secrets of God."

After this, the abbess of Kitzingen,[3] in the diocese of Erfurt, who was her mother's sister, took pity on her in her misery. She took Blessed Elizabeth to her uncle, the Lord Bishop of Bamberg. He had her stay with him and treated her with honor, but also wanted to have her marry again, and this became known to Blessed Elizabeth. Her handmaids, who had vowed continence with her, were afraid that the bishop would use force, and they lamented this with sorrow and tears. Blessed Elizabeth often consoled them, saying, "My faith in God is unshakable. He knows that the vow of chastity, taken in my husband's lifetime, came from a pure and sincere heart. I am confident of his mercy. I know that he will preserve my chastity against any human design, and any kind of violence, because I did not make this vow on condition that it please my friends or provided that God did not reveal some other plan to me—I made an absolute vow [to preserve] total continence after my husband's death. And if my uncle were to give me to another against my will, I would oppose it in word and in spirit. And if I had no other way of escaping, I would cut off my nose in secret. When I am frightfully mutilated like that, no one will trouble any more about me."

However, one day, she was taken against her will to Pottenstein castle, to be kept there until she was wed, as she understood. In tears, she committed her chastity to the Lord, in whom she had placed her heart. And the Lord, the consoler of the afflicted, arranged it so that a messenger came from the bishop ordering her to return to Bamberg to meet her husband's bones, which had been brought back from overseas. When the bones had been solemnly received with a procession by the bishop, she said, weeping, "Lord, I give you thanks for having mercifully consoled me by these bones of my husband which I have so much desired. Great as my love for him was, you know that I do not begrudge the sacrifice that my beloved and I made of himself to you for the liberation of the Holy Land. If I could have him, I would give the whole world for him, and go begging with him forever. But I call upon you to witness that I would not want to redeem his life, even if it cost me but a single hair, if it were against your will. Now I recommend myself and him to your grace. May your will for us be done."

Afterwards she returned to Thuringia with her husband's vassals, who brought his bones for burial to the cloister of the monks of Reinhardsbrunn. The vassals promised that they would arrange for the recovery of her dower. The bishop would not have entrusted her to those nobles unless they guaranteed that they would provide for her comfort. But in fact, after her husband's burial, everyone neglected her interests, and Elizabeth found herself like a beggar again, and in the same poverty as before, until, at the command of Master Conrad, she moved to Marburg.

There she put on a gray tunic, an inexpensive and humble habit. It was also there, at different times, that she gave almost 2,000 marks, which she had received in exchange for her dower, to the poor. On one day she gave 500 marks to countless poor people gathered together. In addition, she distributed to the poor all that remained to her of the jewels which she had brought from the house of her father, the king of Hungary, and everything else that she had. She also founded a hospital in that place. She bore insults, curses and great contempt from the magnates and men of the land, so that her people cared neither to speak to her nor to see her. They thought her foolish and insane, and they insulted her and defamed her in many ways. She bore everything so patiently and with such rejoicing that they even taunted her for it, saying that she had too quickly forgotten her husband's death, and that she rejoiced when she ought to be sad.

And because Master Conrad had persuaded her to have contempt for all things, she begged God first, that he give her contempt for all temporal things, second, that he take away her love of her children, and third, that he inspire in her soul scorn for insults. And after she had poured out her prayer, she said to her handmaids, "God has heard my prayer, and now I look upon the worldly possessions I loved as dung. Likewise, as God is my witness, I am no longer worried about my children, I love them as I love any other neighbor. I have entrusted them to God; let him do with them as he wills. I also rejoice in insults, evil words, and contempt for my person; I love God alone." Master Conrad also tried her constancy in many ways, breaking her will in all things, and ordering her to do what was against her wishes.

So that he could afflict her still more, he deprived her one by one of those members of her household who were particularly dear to her, so that she might suffer inwardly for each one. "And at last," [she said], "he drove me, Isentrude, whom she loved, away from her. She sent me away in great distress and with countless tears. Last of all he removed Guda, my companion, who had lived with her from her childhood, and whom she loved with a special love. The most blessed Elizabeth sent her away with tears and sighs. Master Conrad, of pious memory, did this out of his honest zeal and with this intention: because he feared that we would talk to her of her past glory and that she would be tempted to regret. He also took away from her any comfort she might have in us in this way because he wished her to cling to God alone.

Master Conrad harnessed her to some harsh women from whom she bore many oppressions. They behaved deceptively toward her, as Master Conrad ordered them, and they often reported about her to Master Conrad—when she did not observe obedience, when she gave something to the poor, or when she asked that something be given by others, after she was prohibited by Master Conrad from giving anything. That was because she kept back nothing at all that she did not lavish on the poor. And so, because of the accusations [of these women], she bore many beatings and slaps from Master Conrad, which she desired to bear in memory of the blows in the face Our Lord received. And she was so obedient that she did not dare to give us, that is, Guda and Isentrude, anything at all to eat when we come to see her, or speak to her without permission. She bore with great patience and joy all her adversities, and the contempt people had for her, and a great many beatings, which Master Conrad gave her from his good zeal, so that she might not fall away from her purpose."

When they were questioned under oath, Isentrude and Guda, the said religious women, who were formerly very familiar with Elizabeth when her husband the Landgraf was alive, were in complete agreement about all these things. When they were examined individually, and asked how they knew about what they had said, they declared that they had personally witnessed all these things, and they saw them because they lived with blessed Elizabeth for many years.

Elisabeth, formerly the handmaid of Blessed Elizabeth, the Landgrafin of Thuringia, was put under oath and questioned on Blessed Elizabeth's life and manner of living. She said that after she put on the gray habit, she was with her for a long time, and saw many works of charity in her and she was of great humility. For she called to her hospice, in which she stayed in the town of Marburg the poorest, weakest and sickest and the most devout, to whom she ministered personally. She prepared food with her servants devoted to God in the gray habit and served the poor staying in her hospice, and bathed them and smoothed their beds and covered them. She also had a little one-eyed boy all covered with scabies with her in the hospice. In addition to the great humanity she showed to him, she also often carried him for the necessities of nature.

Irmingard, a religious dressed in the gray habit, formerly the servant of Blessed Elizabeth, when she was put under oath and questioned, said that Blessed Elizabeth used to have poor people in her hospice near the town of Marburg after she was dressed in the gray habit, to whom she ministered by herself. Outside of the hospice, she also gave money with her own hands, so that the poor people might be provided for. And she secretly sold her gold rings and silk robes and other jewels so that she might minister to the poor.

She also said that seven times one night she carried a little one-eyed boy with scabies to attend to the needs of nature. She would frequently carry him to bed and cover him. She also washed the boy's soiled clothes herself, and spoke very cheerfully and gently to him.

She also said that after she built the hospital in Marburg, she helped bathe the sick, and after they were bathed and put into bed, she covered them. One time she tore up a linen curtain with which the building used to be decorated, and spread out the linen cloths for the poor who had been bathed; while she covered them she spoke in this way: "How good for us, that we can bathe and cover Our Lord in this way." And her handmaid answered: "Good for us when we do this? I don't know if others feel like this."

She also said that in the hospital she took care of a leper girl who smelled very badly and was all covered with sores and blood, whom it horrified anyone to see from a distance. Blessed Elizabeth washed her, covered her and bound her sores with cloths, and warmed medications for her. Prostrating herself in front of her, she untied her shoelaces; she also wanted to remove her shoes, but the girl would not permit it. She cut her fingernails and toenails and she touched her face full of sores with her hand, and fittingly, in time she was healed. Elizabeth found a place for her at one end of the courtyard and frequently visited her. At times she called her to her house and played many times with her and smoothed her bed and spoke very gently with that poor little girl and consoled her. And whatever the poor people desired, she eagerly provided for them.

She also used to induce people by exhortations not to neglect to have their children baptized. She also induced sick people to confess so that they might receive Communion. Once she admonished a poor little old woman to go to confession, and when she did not succeed, she beat her with a switch. This woman, who was lying almost asleep and slow to go to confession, did not heed her admonition, and so in this way she compelled her to go, reluctantly, to confession.

After her husband died, Blessed Elizabeth was temporarily not allowed to use her husband's property, because she was prevented from doing so by her husband's brother. She could have received some sustenance from her husband's brother, but she did not want to receive her nourishment by theft and by taxing the poor, as was so often the practice at the courts of princes. She chose to be abject and to earn her bread by the work of her hands like a day-laborer. She acquired food by spinning wool sent to her from the monastery in Altenberg, but—as is known to many—for a price less than was due. She also offered money on the altar which she had acquired by the work of her hands. And Irmingard said that very often when she was sick, lying in bed, she spun wool; indeed she did not know how to spin flax. At times Irmingard took the distaff from her hands, so that she might spare herself. But so that she might not be completely idle, she would pull off wool for future work and spreading it out, prepare it with her hands.

At this same time, she had some large fish that were sent to her sold by Brother Heinrich, the son of the Count of Wegebach —then a hermit, later a brother of the Friars Minor; and the reason why she wanted to sell the fish was so that she might more conveniently provide herself with some money.

It happened, however, that the King of Hungary, Blessed Elizabeth's father, sent a count named Banfy[4] with a large retinue to call his daughter back to her homeland, because he had heard that she was almost a beggar, deprived of all comfort. On coming to the town of Marburg, the count found her seated at the distaff and spinning wool. And crossing himself out of amazement, he said, "Never was a king's daughter seen spinning wool before." And loving, with moderation, all poverty and exile, she could not be induced to return with her father's messenger to the land of her birth.

She had to lengthen her gray habit, which was short, with cloth of other colors. In a similar way, she also had to mend the torn sleeves of her tunic with other colors of cloth. At times also in wintertime, because she did not have enough clothes, she used to lie between two mattresses [on either side], not lying on another mattress or else on the ground. And she spoke these words: "I am lying as though in a coffin," and she rejoiced in tribulation. Blessed Elizabeth was once called by the abbess of

Kitzingen, who was her maternal aunt and who urged her to take a bath. She finally entered the bath with a great deal of noise, placed one foot in the water, and moving it back and forth, said, "This is bathed." And immediately she got out of the tub.

It happened sometimes that when, as has been said, blessed Elizabeth was intent on earning her food by the work of her hands, she was called by Master Conrad to come from Marburg to Eisenach. And because she had received payment [in advance] for spinning wool from the church in Altenberg she sent back one Cologne denier with the wool she had not spun, so that she might not have anything above what was due and that she had not earned by her labor.

Elisabeth, the handmaid of Blessed Elizabeth, after taking the oath, said that a certain noblewoman named Gertrude von Leimbach came to visit Elizabeth. With Gertrude there came a youth named Berthold, dressed in a worldly fashion. Blessed Elizabeth called him to her and said: "You must know that you are not acting at all prudently, and why do you not serve your Creator?" The young man answered, "O, my lady, I beg you to pray for me, so that God may give me His grace, so that I may serve Him." And she said: "Do you want me to pray for you?" And he said: "I certainly do." And she said: "Then you should make yourself fit for the grace of God by praying in the same way, and I will gladly pray for you." And immediately, throwing herself on her knees, as her custom was, in a suitable place in the monastery of Wehrda,[5] in which she then was, she began to pray intently for the young man. The young man, also sought a remote place for prayer in that same monastery. And when both had remained in prayer for some time, the young man began to cry out in a loud voice: "O, lady, lady, stop praying." But she continued to pray fervently. After a short time, the young man began to cry out even more loudly: "O, my lady, stop praying, because I am already growing quite weak." For the young man was sweating all over and steaming from the intense heat, and he threw his arms and his whole body here and there, as though demented. And the lady who was the mistress of the same servant, and the said Elisabeth, the handmaid of Blessed Elizabeth, and Irmingard, who testified to the incident under oath, ran and held on to him, and found him, as Lady Elizabeth said, all hot and drenched with sweat. Again and again he repeated his last cry: "In the name of God, I beg you, stop praying, for I am already being consumed by fire." And those who held him could scarcely bear the heat to their hands. And as soon as Blessed Elizabeth stopped praying, he felt better. And immediately after her death, the young man went over to the Friars Minor. This thing that was said about the young man happened a year before [Elizabeth's] death, and, as the same handmaid Elisabeth said, similar things often happened to other people she prayed for.

When, after much poverty, she received a large sum of money for her dower, she called together the poor and weak within the area of twelve miles from Marburg to a certain place on a certain day and ordered that 500 marks be distributed at one time. And so that everything might be done conveniently and in an orderly way, Blessed Elizabeth herself, with her clothes girded up, went around asking the people to sit down, so that she might pass among them and serve them, following the example of the Lord. And a rule was laid down and it was announced that all those who moved from their place and received alms again, disadvantaging the other poor people and impeding order, would have to suffer the embarrassment of having some of their hair cut off. And it happened right then that a young girl named Hildegunde with very beautiful hair, who was unaware of the said rule, came along. She had not come to receive alms, but to visit her sister who was ill. When this girl was led before Blessed Elizabeth for not observing the rule, so that she might pass judgment on her, and when she saw the beauty of her hair, she ordered that it immediately be cut off. And when the girl, having lost [her hair], began to weep with a loud voice. But some people who knew her to be innocent, came up to Blessed Elizabeth and told her that the young girl should have been punished less severely. And she said to her: "At least in the future, with hair like that, she will not go to dances." And immediately she ordered that the girl be called to her, and asked her if she had ever thought of a better life. And the girl answered that if it hadn't been for her beautiful hair, she would have already been serving God for a long time in the religious habit. And Blessed Elizabeth said to her, "Then you are dearer to me because you have lost your hair than if my son were made emperor." And immediately she received her for all the days of her life for service in the hospital, after she put on the religious habit. She is still serving in the hospital in Marburg today and we have seen her shorn-off hair. Hildegunde stated this under oath, and the parish priest of the town and a number of other people testified to it with her.

On the night following the day on which the 500 marks was generously given as alms, a night with a clear and shining moon, when the stronger of the poor people had left, many of the weaker and the sick remained lying next to the fence enclosing the hospital and in corners of the courtyard. When Blessed Elizabeth entered the courtyard and saw them, she said to those with her, "Look, the weaker ones have remained; let us give them something more." And she ordered that six Cologne deniers be given to each one, and she did not want the children to be given less. Afterwards, she had loaves of bread brought and distributed them to them. When this was done, she said: "We want to make their joy complete, so light some fires for them." And for a long while she had fires prepared, and the feet and nails of many people were washed and anointed with oil. And the poor people began to sing and enjoy themselves. When she heard this, Blessed

Elizabeth said: "You see, I told you that we must make people happy." And she herself rejoiced with those who were rejoicing.

Elisabeth [the handmaid] also stated under oath that when Blessed Elizabeth was in the town of Wehrda,[6] a certain poor woman was there who was close to giving birth, but because her home was remote from that place, Blessed Elizabeth ordered that she should be provided for in a hut next to her house and that the hearth be set in order and a fire made and pillows and cushions and enough covers provided for her. When she had her baby, she had the child baptized and ordered that her own name, [Elizabeth], be given to it and she visited her every day and blessed the child and provided for them for about four weeks. But the poor little woman forgot these benefits when one evening the lady said farewell to her. Blessed Elizabeth gave her a cloak and the shoes from her own feet and 12 Cologne deniers in coin and a robe and ordered that her handmaid, the said Elisabeth, remove her fur sleeves to wrap the child in; she also ordered that bacon and flour be given her.

Very early in the morning, abandoning her child in the house, she left with her husband, to whom [Elizabeth] had also given a pair of shoes. In the morning, when Blessed Elizabeth was in church, before the beginning of Matins, she called her handmaid Elisabeth, and said to her: "I have some money in my purse, which may be useful for comforting that poor little woman and her child. Go and take it to them." When, accordingly, she came to the lodging, where she thought to find the poor little woman, she [discovered that she] had gone and left the child alone in the house. The handmaid returned to Blessed Elizabeth, and told her about the woman's departure, and that she had abandoned her child. Blessed Elizabeth said to her, "Go quickly and bring the child, so it might not be neglected." When it was brought, she entrusted it to the wife of a knight in that village to be taken care of. And immediately she ordered that the city magistrate be called, so that he might send messengers everywhere on all the roads after the child's mother. The messengers returned after a time, having found nothing. Her handmaid Elisabeth informed Blessed Elizabeth of this and begged her to pray that God might show her the child's mother. For she was afraid of Master Conrad, for he would be disturbed at this kind of thing. And she [blessed Elizabeth] said: "I am unable to ask for anything else from God, except that His will be done."

And after an hour, the husband of that poor little woman returned. He threw himself down on the ground before Elizabeth, confessing openly that he found it impossible to continue on with his wife, and that therefore he had come back as though forced. When asked where his wife was, he indicated the exact place and when messengers were sent, she was brought back and she confessed in a similar way, that she was not able to go any farther, and she asked pardon for her very great offense and ingratitude. And when those standing nearby judged that she deserved to be deprived of the cloak and shoes because of her ingratitude and that they should be given to others, so that the cloak and other things of blessed Elizabeth might not be used by someone with a bad reputation, Elizabeth herself said, "Do what you think is right." And the cloak, after being taken from her, was given to a devout virgin in the village, who immediately vowed chastity to the Lord and chose to serve the Lord in the religious habit. The shoes were given to a widow. But, taking pity on that poor little woman, Blessed Elizabeth ordered that other leather clothes and shoes be given to her. She received back the child that she had wickedly abandoned and left.

Irmingard also said that she heard from Blessed Elizabeth: "The life of the sisters in the world is the most despised, and if there were a more despised life, I would have chosen it. I could have promised obedience to some of the bishops or abbots who have possessions, but I thought it better to promise it to Master Conrad, who does not have anything, but who is a complete beggar, so that I might have absolutely no consolation in this life." She also said that Blessed Elizabeth used to fear Master Conrad very much, but in place of God, saying, "If I fear a mortal man so much, how much more to be feared is Almighty God, who is the Lord and Judge of all."

Irmingard also said that Master Conrad once ordered Blessed Elizabeth to come to Altenberg, so that she might receive his advice as to whether he would place her in a recluse's cell. And the cloistered ladies asked this of Master Conrad, that when Blessed Elizabeth came, he would give her permission to enter the cloister so that they might see her. And Master Conrad answered, "Let her enter, if she wants to," actually believing that she would not enter. She entered nonetheless, believing she had permission, trusting in the previous words of Master Conrad. On learning this, Master Conrad called Blessed Elizabeth and reprimanding her, showed her the prepared book, so that she might swear to obey his order, on account of the excommunication she had incurred by entering the cloister. And although Sister Irmingard had only stood outside, because outside she had accepted the key and opened the door of the cloister, he told her to prostrate herself with Blessed Elizabeth and ordered Brother Gerard to beat them soundly with a very thick rod. Meanwhile Master Conrad sang *Misere mei Deus*.[7] And the said Irmingard said that after three weeks she still had the marks of the beating, and Blessed Elizabeth, who had been more severely beaten, had even more.

And Irmingard said that after Blessed Elizabeth bore such things, she heard from her: "We must bear such things gladly, for it is with us as it is with the grass growing in the river: when the river is rising, the grass is beaten down and flattened, and the flood waters pass over it without doing it any harm. When the flood is over, the grass stands upright and grows in its vigor, joyfully and delightedly. We should do the same when it is necessary: bend and humble ourselves, and afterwards stand up joyfully and gladly."

Irmingard also said about Blessed Elizabeth that she was so circumspect that she sought out a doctor from time to time to give her a diet so that she might not perhaps take away too much from herself and incur illness from the undue deprivation, which would take her away from obedience to God, and so she might have to answer to God for too much abstinence. Also, she did not want to be called "lady" by her handmaids, who were very poor and low-born, but only the [familiar] singular "Thou, Elizabeth." And she had her handmaids sit next to her and eat from her dish. One time, the handmaid Irmingard said: "You acquire merit for yourself through us, but you don't pay any attention to our misfortune, that we might become proud because we are eating with you and sitting beside you." At this Blessed Elizabeth said: "Well, then, thou must sit in my lap," and she made Irmingard sit in her lap.

Irmingard said that Blessed Elizabeth washed earthenware pots, plates and dishes and very often sent the handmaids away so that she might not be prohibited by them from doing this kind of work. Very often, when they came back they found her busy washing the dishes and other utensils. At times also, they found the washing done.

Blessed Elizabeth also went with her handmaids to the homes of the poor and brought with her bread and meat and other food to give to the poor and she gave it with her own hands and carefully saw to the clothes and beds of the poor. And on her return, she would be absorbed in prayer, and she used to very devoutly honor the relics of the saints with lighted incense and candles. She also used to give many things to the poor at the same time, and when she accepted the command from Master Conrad, she no longer gave them several deniers at once, but rather one; she was careful to give them out one at a time, because she was not allowed to give them at the same time. When Master Conrad heard this, he ordered her not to give any more money, but bread. But she gave a large amount of bread at once, as before. So he then ordered her to give only little pieces of bread. And she was prompt to obey him in everything. That is why, when Master Conrad once ordered her to return as she was on her way to visit a certain hermit, she answered the messenger: "We are like turtles, who withdraw into their shells when it rains; so too with us, when we obey, we withdraw from the way that we had begun to go."

Blessed Elizabeth also ordered that her child, who was a year and a half old, be completely removed from her, so that she might not love her too much and that she might not be impeded for her sake from serving God.

Irmingard also said of Blessed Elizabeth that when she was most joyful, she wept most. That is to say, she was seen to rejoice and weep at the same time, and when she wept, her face never changed through lines, wrinkles or deformity, but tears flowed down her face as though from a fountain, very serenely and joyfully. This is why she said of those who distorted their faces in weeping, "They seem almost to frighten the Lord; let them give to God what they have with joy and cheerfulness."

When she came to a cloister of religious who did not have property, but who were fed much from alms every day, they showed her sumptuous carvings in relief covered with gold in their church. While about twenty-four of those religious were gathered around her, she said: "Look, better for you to have placed this expense in your clothes and food than in walls, because you should carry this sculptured image in your heart." For this reason, when someone said to her of some beautiful picture, that it was suitable for her, she answered, "I don't need such a picture, because I carry it in my heart."

She was very cheerful and patient, rejoicing in tribulation, and she was never seen to suffer from annoyance. She could not bear to have useless and angry words spoken in her presence, because she would immediately say, "Where is God now?"

And although we could put into writing a number of things of this kind about her sanctity, humility, patience and discretion, that we understood from those who were around her, in order to avoid going on at too great a length, we will set down something about her end. Elisabeth, the handmaid of the Lady Landgrafin, said: "When my lady, Blessed Elizabeth was lying in her bed for the last time, I heard a very sweet voice, as though in her throat, and she was lying turned towards the wall. After a time, turning to me, she said: 'Where are you, dear?' I said, 'Here I am.' And I added: 'Oh, my lady, how sweetly you sing.' And she asked whether I had heard it, and I said yes. And she said: 'I tell you that between me and the wall, a little bird was singing very merrily, and I was so stirred by its voice that I had to sing too.' This happened several days before her death." The same handmaid also said: "My lady, blessed Elizabeth, always spoke very merry words to us handmaids, calling us 'dear' or 'friend.'

"Also, when we were seated around Blessed Elizabeth as she lay in bed for the last time, she said to us: 'What shall we do if the devil shows himself to us?' After a short time she cried in a loud voice, as though expelling the demon: 'Go away, go away, go away,' and she said: 'Now we should be speaking of God and the Child Jesus, because it is now near midnight, when Jesus was born and lay in the manger, and he created his new star with the greatest power, such as was never seen by anyone before.' And speaking like this she was very cheerful, as if she were not sick. And she said: 'Although I am weak, I do not feel ill at all.'"

The handmaid Irmingard also said that before her death, she also heard Blessed Elizabeth say: "Now the time is drawing near when Almighty God will call his friends." And she said that all that day, which was the one before her death, she was filled with great devotion. And at the very hour of her death, she lay back as though she were sleeping, and expired.

And although Blessed Elizabeth's body lay unburied until the fourth day after the hour of her death, it gave off absolutely no fetid odor, as is usual with others; on the contrary it had a sweet fragrance, which seemed to refresh the spirit. Her body was dressed in a gray tunic and her face bound with pieces of cloth. Several people, enflamed by devotion, cut off pieces of the cloth, others tore or cut the hair from her head and cut off her fingernails and toenails. Some other women also mutilated her ears. Others also cut off the tips of her breasts and kept them for themselves in this way for relics. But how great was the sorrow of the crowd of the poor who had heard of her death; she was a mother to all; it is difficult to explain individual sorrow and ways of behaving.

When vigils were being sung, the abbess of Wetter, who was then present, heard little birds singing very joyfully. Wondering where this might be, she went outside the church and saw many little birds gathered together on the church spire, and heard them sing in their different ways, as though they were performing Elizabeth's funeral rites. And though we might write many things that we have seen and understood about her life and conduct and devotion and about her hospital in Marburg and the very virtuous management of the sick and poor in the same hospital, and the covering of silk and several shades of purple there, to avoid going on at too great a length, we have ordered that only some of the many things be written down.

❧

Testimonies from

The Anonymous Franciscan

The testimonies here have been arranged roughly following the chronological order of Elizabeth's life. Occasionally it is clear that the Anonymous Franciscan has added some words of his own to the originals, and I have indicated these as much as possible, but the substance of the testimonies appears to be much as the original witnesses gave them.

Franciscan Brother Andrew of Westphalia

The Anonymous Franciscan describes Brother Andrew as "a man of praiseworthy memory, who devoted himself to the Roman emperor Frederick in many great and difficult matters before he entered the order and stood by him as a confidential and salutary counselor for a long time and in many different parts of the world. He was commonly considered famous and celebrated as a man adorned with learning in Holy Scripture, and in both canon and civil law, and, before he was questioned about these things, he refused the episcopate that had been offered to him." The testimony seems to have been expanded somewhat with the Anonymous Franciscan's own comments about the friar's role. This passage is part of the description of events following Elizabeth's expulsion from her dower castle.

Brother Andrew of Westphalia . . . answered the investigators that at that time blessed Elizabeth had arrived at such temporal need and at such straits of total deprivation of everything that there was no one left of all her loved ones to console her. When this Friar Minor saw the daughter of the king of Hungary, duchess of the Thuringians, and Landgrafin not only destitute of all help and solace, but even exposed to uncommon abuse and oppression, after having a conversation with some discreet brothers he diligently devised what might be done. They saw that they were not able to protect her or defend her from her adversaries, and hoped that Master Conrad of Marburg would suffice for the relief and protection of the servant of God Elizabeth, because at that time the apostolic authority had raised him in a way around those parts against the heretics. So they advised her to commit herself to the guidance of the said Master Conrad and subject herself completely to his teaching. The humble daughter consented without delay to the advice of the brothers, and from then on humbly obeyed him. But after a long time had passed, Master Conrad was able neither to defend her nor to cause what was hers to be restored to her; rather, the most recent events for the holy servant of God went from bad to worse. Since he was unable to do this himself, the Friar Minor, with compassionate tenderness, urgently asked and obtained permission from his superiors, and set out for the Roman Curia. Divine clemency was immediately generous to him when he asked for apostolic letters from the Lord Leo, Cardinal of the Roman See, who was his familiar friend, with whom he had stayed for a long time while at school, and with whom he had lived constantly together in one house. With these as his authority, the brother, like a faithful steward, hastened to meet with the adversaries of poor Elizabeth, manfully constraining them both by threats and by entreaties. In the end, they restored to the poor unhappy widow what was hers and brought her back as lady to her own [property]. They also paid her five hundred marks sterling for the remainder of her dower. After distributing half of it to the poor, she generously gave the remainder for the completion of the buildings in the hospital of blessed Francis. In this way, the strong Lord, the Lord powerful in battle (Ps 23:8) chose the weak things of the world to confound the strong (Cf. 1 Cor. 1:27), and through the simple, poor and humble Friar Minor, those who could in no way be called back from evil by fear of God were coerced by the severity of ecclesiastical discipline.

Testimonies about Elizabeth's Clothing in Marburg

This passage gives us more information about Elizabeth's clothing in Marburg than can be found in Isentrude's testimony. It too apparently comes from the canonization process, though the names of individual witnesses are not given. The fact that the Franciscan guardian of Hesse is described as tonsuring and clothing Elizabeth, agrees with the statement of Isentrude that this event took place in Marburg in Hesse.

Certain people also testified at that time that Brother Burchard, the guardian of the Friars Minor of Hesse, in the presence of Brother Henry, called Placido, of the same order, happily tonsured her, as his dearest daughter and spiritual friend, and clothed her after her husband's death, while Master Conrad celebrated Mass at that time in the place [of the friars].

Franciscan Brother Gerard from beyond the Alps

The Anonymous Franciscan adds some words to his account of this deposition to indicate that Gerard testified both in the first investigation of 1233 and the second (and last) one of 1235, but he apparently confuses the two in the last paragraph.

A contemporary of blessed Elizabeth, her faithful friend, brother Gerard from beyond the Alps, of the order of Friars Minor, was questioned about these things in the second and last inquiry about the acts of the same servant of God diligently made by great, learned and authoritative persons. At that time he had gone to that place out of love for the humble Elizabeth, and had visited that hospital of the poor which she had built in the name of blessed Francis. When he was questioned both in the first and the last investigation, in the presence of many great men, varying in nothing, he answered several times that she was of such profound humility that after her husband's death she commonly went about in a shabby tunic, which was patched, especially in the sleeves, girded with a quite rough cord, covered with a mantle with many patches and lengthened with cloth of another color, like another abbess Clare of the cloistered sisters. The same brother also firmly declared that he also saw another noblewoman, a relative of the Roman Emperor Frederick, with whom he had a conversation for one whole day over many things pertaining to salvation, who followed the life of blessed Elizabeth in a cord and habit as abject as it was humble. She went around barefoot, and actually asked just as faithfully as humbly for the alms necessary for herself from the Friars Minor. The same brother declared that he saw a large number of other very noble women living in a very similar way, with whom he had many salutary conversations and visits about these and other matters. It was also declared at that time in that second investigation, and

152

diligently redacted in writing, and it was also found in the last investigation that blessed Elizabeth was led by such ardor of devotion towards the name of blessed Francis that out of her desire [and] very great love, she used an impression in the likeness of some Friars Minor as a seal on many of her letters.

Other Testimonies on Elizabeth's Habit

Those questioned about these or other things previously mentioned included not only Brother Gerard, but also several other religious and lay people. Several of these men and women remained at one time or another with her or were her familiar friends or were devoted to her almost as long as she lived. In addition, three brothers of the Order of Preachers, namely, brother Jacobus from beyond the Alps, brother Dietrich of Malburg,[1] and brother Johannes from near Kempen,[2] gave testimony to the truth one by one. One testified especially about her cord, and the other two about her habit, just as they saw and heard concerning these things.

Franciscan Brother Gerard of Geldern

For one day the man of all honesty and prudence, Brother Gerard of Geldern, minister of the order of Friars Minor of Upper Germany,[3] the father and special confessor of blessed Elizabeth, who was more intimate with her and had more influence over her than anyone after Master Conrad, talked with her about the priceless treasure of precious poverty. The saint answered, like one who was no longer of this world, "Since it is a question about holy poverty for me, I desire with all my heart that at the crossroads outside the walls a cell should be made for me of muddy straw and earth, and that in front of the little door or window a linen thread should be tied, and a small container hung on it, in which passersby would put alms to sustain me in a transitory way, as it is customary to do for poor lepers." And after saying these things in a vehement spirit, she was wondrously carried away and elevated above herself, and her slight body suddenly fell as though unconscious into the most devout arms of the said minister, her sweetest father. At last, coming back to herself, she began to breathe a little, praising and blessing the King of Heaven. The same minister, when he was asked where this saint was, answered that she was in the hospital of St. Francis in Marburg.

࿐

The Bull of Canonization:

Gloriosus in Majestate

June 1, 1235

Gregory, bishop, servant of the servants of God, to our venerable brothers, the archbishops and bishops, and to our beloved sons, the abbots, priors, archdeacons, priests, deacons, and other prelates of churches to whom this letter is delivered: greetings and apostolic blessing.

Glorious in his majesty, the son of the eternal Father, our Lord and Redeemer, Jesus Christ, looked down from the height of heaven and saw the glory of the human condition disfigured by the great confluence of misery begun by the sin of our first parents. In his ineffable providence, he made ready both to reveal his power to those seated in the shadow of death, and to recall those in exile to the homeland of liberty. No one was better fitted than he for the redemption of his handiwork—for if by chance a craftsman's work is ruined, it is fitting and proper for him to discern how to shape it more beautifully, and by his power to restore it devotedly to its pristine state. And so he went from his royal throne into a slender little vessel, which, although small, received a guest more vast than all others, that is, the womb of

155

the Virgin, filled with every abundance of holiness. He brought forth from it a work visible to all, through which, when he had driven back the prince of darkness, he triumphed in the redemption of his created image. He left behind sure principles for the faithful, through which a free passage might be made for them to their homeland.

Now Blessed Elizabeth, the offspring of a royal line, and the gracious Landgrafin of Thuringia, weighed such an unbroken series of mercies, and in attentive meditation, chose to observe these principles with constant devotion, in order to make herself worthy to see perpetual light. She gave herself to the cultivation of these virtues, from the rising of her life until its setting, you might say, never ceasing to find her joy in embracing charity. For just as she confessed the true faith, and devoted her mind to holiness, and as she loved the Son of the Queen of Heaven, through whom she was able to receive the sweetness of celestial nuptials, she also loved her neighbors.

For she delighted in the familiar presence of those whose unpleasant corruption made all others want to stay far away from them, and she went without many things so that she might be lavish in many ways in her solicitude for the poor. From her most tender age, she wanted to be their protector and friend, for she knew that the reward of everlasting life, the reward of those dear to God, is acquired through the merits of the poor, so their condition, naturally despised by the pride of the world, was a pleasure to her. For she gave many proofs of her dislike for even the legitimate pleasures which her high rank by marriage offered her, and, frequently shunning these things in contempt she caused her tender and delicate body to waste away through her constant zeal for abstinence. She succeeded in obtaining for herself the greater quantity of merit, for whatever is done voluntarily is honored with the reward of greater grace. What more is there to say? Transforming every right of her blood into a desire for heavenly delight, she looked upon it as an imperfection, once she was left to pass the rest of her life deprived of the protection of her husband, not to confine herself in the yoke of obedience, which she had already embraced while under her husband's authority without prejudice to him. She clothed herself in the religious habit, in which she did not fail until her last day to celebrate within herself the mystery of the Passion of the Lord.

Oh happy woman! Oh wondrous wife! Oh sweet Elizabeth (which means "satisfaction of God")! By nourishing the poor, she deserved the bread of the angels! Oh glorious widow, fertile in offspring of virtues, who was eager to obtain by grace what could not be granted by nature, and who subdued the cruel enemies of the soul by the shield of faith, the breastplate of justice, the sword of the spirit, the helmet of salvation, and the spear of perseverance! Thus she made herself lovable to the immortal Spouse. Thus she united herself to the Queen of virgins in a steadfast love, and reduced her lordship to the servitude of an humble handmaid. Thus Elizabeth conformed herself to the ways of olden days by walking in the laws and just ordinances of the Lord simply and without complaint. She conceived through love the grace of God in the secret of her soul, brought it to fruition by her acts and nourished it by her constant progress to such a point that the Lord, the support of souls hoping in him, who exalts all who dwell in the valleys of humility and innocence, rose up to give her the reward promised to his faithful. Freeing her from the bonds of death, he carried her to his luminous throne in inaccessible light.

And so it has come to pass that from this stupendous and inexplicable brightness her spirit both shines in the endless depths of heavenly radiance and gleams in this profound darkness by the many glorious miracles, by virtue of which Catholics receive an increase of faith, hope, and charity, the way to truth is pointed out to unbelievers, and material accumulated for the confusion of the heretics, who were enveloped in the coils of pride. For by the merits of the saint who, while enclosed in the prison of the flesh, was poor in spirit, meek of mind, wept over her sins or rather the sins of others, thirsted after justice, dedicated herself to mercy, was pure of heart, truly peace-loving and crushed by abuse and persecutions, these heretics see life restored to the dead, sight to the blind, hearing to the deaf, speech to the dumb and the power of walking to the sick, by the right hand of heaven. They see the vast regions of Germany which they have tried to poison by their doctrine of death exult in many ways in the embrace of heavenly doctrine.

Testimony on these and other similar miracles worked by the saint—which offer more abundant joy when inspected with the eyes of the mind than when they are seen spread out elegantly adorned in writing—has been given to us by suitable witnesses with the most complete fidelity, as is due and fitting for respect for truth in all things. Since we are required by our office to constantly exert ourselves in study of those things by which the glory of the Redeemer may be increased, with the advice and assent of our brothers [the cardinals], and our brothers the venerable Patriarchs, Archbishops, Bishops and all the other prelates who at that time were at the Apostolic See, we have thought it right that this holy woman, whom He has pleased to receive into the contemplation of his majesty, be inserted into the catalogue of the saints. We order all of you by this apostolic letter and strictly enjoin you to celebrate her feast day and have it solemnly celebrated as much as the greatness of her marvelous merits demands, on November 19,[1] that is, on the day when, freed from the bonds of death, passing to everlasting life, she proceeded to the source of heavenly delight.

This was so that there might come to us through her devout intercession from the heavenly treasury that delight which, standing before Christ, she is known to perceive and glories in possessing eternally. Moreover, by the authority granted to us from on high, through the mercy of the Lord, for the whole of the faithful who are pursuing the delights of the invisible court, and in order to exalt the name of the Most High in having the venerable tomb of his bride honored by their approach, full of trust in the mercy of the Almighty, by the authority of his blessed Apostles, Saint Peter and Saint Paul, we mercifully grant release from a year and forty days of the penance imposed on them to all those who, truly penitent and having confessed, go there each year on the abovementioned feast day and during the whole octave, bearing fragrant signs of devotion and sincerity.

Given at Perugia, on first day of June, in the ninth year of our pontificate.

Part III

Celebrating a Saint in Prayer

❧

Prayers

A Litany to Saint Elizabeth

This litany is based on one used by the Third Order nuns in Lyon in the nineteenth century.

Lord, have mercy on us.
Christ, have mercy on us.
Lord, have mercy on us.
Christ, hear us.
Christ, graciously hear us.
God the Father in Heaven,
have mercy on us.
God the Son, Redeemer of the world,
have mercy on us.
God the Holy Spirit,
have mercy on us.
Holy Trinity, One God,
have mercy on us.

R: Pray for us.

Holy Mary, Mother of Mercy, pray for us.
Holy Elizabeth, mother of the poor,

Saint Elizabeth, who feared God from your heart,

Saint Elizabeth, most fervent in devotion,

Saint Elizabeth, devout and beloved disciple of Jesus,

Saint Elizabeth, imitator of blessed Francis,

Saint Elizabeth, of noblest faith and birth,

Saint Elizabeth, devoted to all pious offices,

Saint Elizabeth, whose nights were spent in prayer and
      contemplation,

Saint Elizabeth, who was consoled with heavenly visions,

Saint Elizabeth, beloved of God and man,

Saint Elizabeth, full of contempt for worldly things,

Saint Elizabeth, example of poverty, chastity, and obedience,

Saint Elizabeth, solace of your husband,

Saint Elizabeth, mirror of widows,

Saint Elizabeth, holocaust of penance and humility,

Saint Elizabeth, admirable preacher of meekness,

Saint Elizabeth, despiser of the luxuries of the regal house,

Saint Elizabeth, lover of the Cross of Christ,

Saint Elizabeth, light of all pious women,

Saint Elizabeth, nourisher of orphans,

Saint Elizabeth, always intent on works of mercy,

Saint Elizabeth, consoler of all sorrows,

Saint Elizabeth, teacher of the poor,

Saint Elizabeth, patient bearer of insults and injuries,

Saint Elizabeth, distributor of your riches to your poor
      neighbors,

Saint Elizabeth, patient in adversity,

Saint Elizabeth, maker of garments for the poor,

Saint Elizabeth, hospitable receiver of pilgrims and the sick,

Saint Elizabeth, succor of the needy,

Saint Elizabeth, formidable to demons,

Saint Elizabeth, example of all spiritual perfection,

Saint Elizabeth, repressor of all vain and dissolute conversation,

Saint Elizabeth, cheered by angelic choirs in your last agony,
Saint Elizabeth, miraculous in life,
Saint Elizabeth, helper of our devotions,
Saint Elizabeth, our sweetest patron,

Lamb of God, You take away the sins of the world,
Spare us, O Lord.
Lamb of God, You take away the sins of the world,
Graciously hear us, O Lord.
Lamb of God, You take away the sins of the world,
Have mercy on us.
Christ, hear us.
Christ, graciously hear us.
V. Pray for us, blessed Elizabeth,
R. That we may be made worthy of the promises of Christ.
V. Let Us Pray.

O God of tender mercies, pour forth Your light over the hearts of Your faithful people, and graciously listening to the glorious prayers of blessed Elizabeth, lead us to think little of worldly prosperity and to be ever gladdened by heavenly consolation; through Our Lord Jesus Christ, who lives and reigns with God the Father and the Holy Spirit, world without end.
R. Amen.

A Short Litany to St. Elizabeth

This litany is addressed to the saint as Protector of the Third Order Franciscans

Lord, have mercy on us.
Christ, have mercy on us.
Lord, have mercy on us.

O Christ, hear us.

O Christ, graciously hear us.

O God the Father in heaven: have mercy on us.

O God the Son, Redeemer of the world: have mercy on us.

O God, the Holy Spirit: have mercy on us.

O Holy Trinity, one God: have mercy on us.

Holy Mary: Pray for us.

Immaculate Virgin: Mother and Mistress of our Order: Pray for us.

St. Elizabeth, Princess of Hungary: Pray for us.

St. Elizabeth, Duchess of Thuringia: Pray for us.

St. Elizabeth, mother in Israel: Pray for us.

St. Elizabeth, queen in the Kingdom of God: Pray for us.

St. Elizabeth, consoler of sinners: Pray for us.

St. Elizabeth, nurse of lepers: Pray for us.

St. Elizabeth, devoted wife of Louis the Good: Pray for us.

St. Elizabeth, famous exemplar of Christian widowhood: Pray for us.

St. Elizabeth, fervent spouse of the Son of God: Pray for us.

St. Elizabeth, humble in prosperity: Pray for us.

St. Elizabeth, patient in adversity: Pray for us.

St. Elizabeth, mighty in penance: Pray for us.

St. Elizabeth, wondrous in prayer: Pray for us.

St. Elizabeth, protectress of our Order: Pray for us.

St. Elizabeth, the "dear saint" of our Holy Church: Pray for us.

O Lamb of God, You take away the sins of the world: spare us, O Lord.

O Lamb of God, You take away the sins of the world: graciously hear us, O Lord.

O Lamb of God, You take away the sins of the world: have mercy on us.

V. Pray for us, O blessed Elizabeth. Alleluia.

R. That we may be made worthy of the promises of Christ.
Alleluia.

Let us pray: Merciful Lord, we ask You to pour the bright beams of Your grace into our hearts: so that, by the glorious prayers of Your Saint Elizabeth, we may learn to despise all worldly prosperity, and ever to rejoice in all Heavenly consolation.
Through Christ our Lord.
Amen.

Prayers to St. Elizabeth

O Saint Elizabeth, model of every sublime virtue, through your example you showed the world how charity, faith and humility can transform a Christian soul.

You loved God with an ardor so intense that He allowed you to experience on earth the joys of heaven. With your invincible faith you were a true disciple of the Gospel. Because you saw Jesus Christ himself in your neighbor, you found great joy in talking with the poor, serving them, drying their tears and coming to their aid.

Your humility was so great that you exchanged your throne for a miserable hut, and your royal mantle for the modest habit of St. Francis. You then subjected yourself, though innocent, to a life of privations and penitence, joyfully embracing the cross of the Divine Redeemer.

O Saint Elizabeth, be the celestial friend of our souls.

Help us love Jesus as you loved him. Protect us on our difficult pilgrimage and obtain for us forgiveness for our sins. Open the way for us to where you sit among the blessed in the kingdom of heaven. Amen.

*****

Saint Elizabeth, noble in your birth and more noble in your rebirth, listen to us pilgrims of the third millennium.

You were among the first disciples of Francis of Assisi. From the first Franciscans you learned love for Christ present in the poor. They initiated you into a life of humility, chastity and obedience. Obtain for us your certainty of the presence of Christ in our brothers and sisters who are being crucified by so many spiritual and physical infirmities.

You were an affectionate wife and mother: obtain for us too a sensitive and courteous charity.

You underwent difficult trials in your life with perfect joy: obtain for us the gifts of joy and peace even in adversity.

In your widowhood you dedicated yourself entirely to the service of God and the poor. Help all faithful lay people and those in consecrated life shine in the Church through their witness to the Gospel and through their intimacy with God.

Through consciously accepted obedience, you learned to bend your will to God's will. Lead us in the same direction.

Though you were rich, you became poor in order to enrich many with your charity. Though a noble princess, you did not let yourself be seduced by luxury and vanity. Teach us inner freedom so that we might be attentive to the Word of God and the needs of our brothers and sisters.

In your labor of service in your hospital of St. Francis, you became everything for everyone. Yet you preserved your spirit of peace and the ability to make people happy. Help us obtain the spirit of blessing and praise, grateful for the gifts that we continuously receive from divine generosity. Amen.

Notes

Part I

Foreword

[1] This beautiful characterization is from Gábor Klaniczay, *Holy Rulers and Blessed Princesses: Dynastic Cults in Medieval Central Europe*, translated by Éva Pálmai (New York: Cambridge University Press, 2002), p. 420.

A Note on the Sources

[1] There is an excellent discussion of the relationship between the sources in Ancelet-Hustache, *Gold Tried by Fire: St. Elizabeth of Hungary* (Chicago: Franciscan Herald Press, 1963), pp. ix-xxx. See also Lori Pieper, *St. Elizabeth of Hungary: The Voice of a Medieval Woman* (Loretto PA: Franciscan Friars TOR, 2007), pp. 21-95.

[2] Lori Pieper, SFO, "A New Life of St. Elizabeth of Hungary: The Anonymous Franciscan," published in *Archivum Franciscanum Historicum* 93 (2000): 29-78.

Prologue: A Turbulent World

[1] Dante Alighieri *Il Convivio* [The Banquet], IV, xxviii, 9-10.

[2] II Celano VI, 10.

Chapter 1: From Hungary to Germany

[1] The exact place of Elizabeth's birth has long been disputed. From the eighteenth century on, many German historians assumed that she was born in Pressburg, or Poszony (now Bratislava, the capital of Slovakia), because this was a residence much favored by Andrew II and his wife, and was also the place from which Elizabeth departed on her trip to Germany at her betrothal. Most historians now follow the late fifteenth-century Hungarian Franciscan, Pelbart of Temesvar, who says that she was born in Sárospatak; this local tradition is in accordance with the circumstances in her family at the time of her birth.

[2] Franciscan writers of the thirteenth century are the first to transmit the legendary "miracle of the roses" to us; the earliest account is dated about 1250, and comes from a manuscript of the Biblioteca Laurenziana in Florence. I have followed the similar version in the Anonymous Franciscan, from around 1300.

[3] Some historians think that Elizabeth was betrothed first to another of the Landgraf's sons, Hermann, who they believe was the oldest, and that only after Hermann's untimely death at the age of fifteen or sixteen was she betrothed to Ludwig. There is no credible evidence for this belief, as Ludwig is always considered in the early sources as the oldest son. See Jeanne Ancelet-Hustache, *Gold Tried by Fire*: *St. Elizabeth of Hungary* (Chicago: Franciscan Herald Press, 1963), p. 39.

[4] Dietrich of Apolda, *Vita*, I, 2.

[5] "Legende von Sant Elsebetenn," *Passional oder der Heiligen Leben* (Strassburg: J. Knoblauch, 1517, 1521). Montalembert believed that this work was written in the fourteenth century because it used an earlier form of German; see his *Histoire de Ste. Elisabeth de Hongrie, duchesse de Thuringe* (Paris, Lecoffre, 1861), p. 163.

Chapter II: Elizabeth's Childhood

[1] Translated in Barbara Newman, *God and the Goddesses: Vision, Poetry and Belief in the Middle Ages* (Philadelphia: University of Pennsylvania Press, 2003), p. 178.

[2] Klaniczay, *Holy Rulers and Blessed Princesses*, pp. 247-48.

[3] Lori Pieper, St. Elizabeth of Hungary and the Franciscan Tradition," Ph.D. dissertation in history, Fordham University (New York, 2002), pp. 414-15.

[4] Dietrich, *Vita*, III, 1.

[5] Dietrich, *Vita*, I, 5.

Chapter III: Marriage and Children

[1] It is mentioned in the "Cronica Reinhards-brunnensis," ed. O. Holder-Egger, *Monumenta Germaniae Historica. Scriptores* 30 (1896): 589.

[2] Dietrich, *Vita*, I, 7.

[3] The document is in Otto Posse and Hubert Ermisch, eds. *Codex diplomaticus Saxoniae Regiae*, 1 Haupteil, III Band (Leipzig, 1898), No. 293, p. 213. In it, Ludwig calls her "Our lady (*domne*), Landgrafin Elizabeth."

[4] *Gaudium et Spes*, no. 48.

[5] Caesarius of Heisterbach, "*Vita Sancte Elyzabeth*," Ed. A. Huyskens, in A. Hilka ed., *Die Wundergeschichten des Caesarius von Heisterbach* (Bonn, 1937), vol. 3, p. 354.

[6] Walther, *Walther von der Vogelweide, the Single-Stanza Lyrics*, ed. Frederick Goldin (New York: Routlege, 2003), pp. 244-45.

[7] I have used examples of the rite from German liturgical manuscripts from the twelfth and thirteenth centuries, which would have been similar to the those Elizabeth participated in; they can be found in Adolf Franz, *Die kirchlichen Benediktionen im Mittelalter* (Graz: Akademische Druck- und Verlagsanstalt, 1960), vol. II, pp. 213-21.

[8] Dietrich, *Vita*, III, 12.

[9] Dietrich, *Vita*, II, 7.

Chapter IV: The Minstrels of God

[1] I owe this thought, as well as so much else, to Fr. Fernando Scocca, TOR.

[2] Giordano of Giano, *Chronicle*, no. 25.

[3] Nicholas Glassberger, a Franciscan chronicler of the sixteenth century, says that Elizabeth "often visited" the foundation established by Giordano on this occasion; "De fratrum minorum ordinis origine," *Analecta ad Fratrum Minorum Historiam* (Leipzig, 1882), p. 37. It is regrettable we don't know more about these first foundations in Thuringia, and that Giordano didn't tell us more about Elizabeth's part in the establishment.

[4] It has long been known that a friary was built in Marburg in 1233, after Elizabeth's death, but some historians have doubted the existence of an earlier Franciscan foundation in the town. There are a number of overlooked sources, however, that

document the earlier foundation, which, like many of the first lodgings of the friars, was outside the city walls. For more on this question, see Pieper, *St. Elizabeth of Hungary: The Voice of a Medieval Woman and Franciscan Penitent in the Sources for Her Life* (Loretto, PA: Franciscan Friars TOR, 2007), pp. 157-160.

[5] Francis of Assisi *Letter to All the Faithful*, I, 1, 4, 10. (The longer redaction of a letter to the Brothers and Sisters of Penance).

[6] Pieper, "St. Elizabeth of Hungary and the Franciscan Tradition," p. 440.

[7] Dietrich, *Vita*, III, 3.

Chapter V: Master Conrad

[1] Caesarius, *Vita*, no. 4; in Hilka, *Wundergeschichte*, p. 351.

[2] Giordano, *Chronicle*, nos. 28 and 30.

[3] Caesarius of Heisterbach, *Vita*, no. 5 in Hilka, *Wundergeschichte*, pp. 353-54.

[4] Mechtild of Magdeburg, *The Flowing Light of the Godhead*, Pt. II. Chap. 25.

Chapter VI: The Mother of the Poor

[1] The Latin text of the document is in Posse and Ermisch, *Codex diplomaticus Saxoniae Regiae*, No. 309, p. 221.

[2] Weigelt, Sylvia, *Thüringen um 1200* (Erfurt: Landeszentrale für politische Bildung, 2007), p. 69.

[3] Weigelt, loc., cit, p. 70.

[4] André Vauchez, "Charité et pauvreté chez Sainte Elisabeth de Thuringe, d'après les actes du procès de canonisation," in Michel Mollat, ed., *Études sur l'histoire de la pauvreté* (Paris, 1974), I, pp. 163-73.

Chapter VII: The Crusader's Cross

[1] Caesarius, "Vita Sancte Elyzabeth," no. 5, in Hilka, *Die Wundergeschichten,* p. 354.

[2] Dietrich, *Vita*, IV, 2 (b).

[3] Dietrich, *Vita*, IV, 3.

[4] Dietrich, *Vita*, IV, 5.

[5] Dietrich, *Vita*, IV, 6. The scene of Elizabeth receiving her husband's ring after his death was one of the earliest to be included in cycles of art works on her life; it is among the scenes on the shrine in her church in Marburg and in the stained glass windows of the church, which was built between 1240 and 1250 with support from her family. These versions show Elizabeth receiving the ring directly from messengers. Dietrich does not mention the ring in his version of this scene, so we don't know exactly how it fits in. It is possible that the messenger carrying the ring arrived after the family had learned of Ludwig's death through other means, but I think that the way I have portrayed the scene is a quite probable one.

Chapter VIII: "Lord, I Want to Be With You"

[1] See Huyskens, *Quellenstudien*, pp. 95-96.

[2] Caesarius, "*Vita*," no. 14, lines 21-22; Hilka, Die *Wundergeschichte*, p. 363.

[3] *The Little Flowers of St. Francis* (*Fioretti*), Chapter VIII.

Chapter IX: The Beloved Bones

[1] Dietrich, *Vita*, V, 7-9.

[2] Dietrich, *Vita*, VIII, 17. Also in miracles of canonization process (1235, no. 24).

[3] In fact, as Irmingard's testimony indicates, even after she established her hospital, Conrad thought of having her become a recluse.

Chapter X: The Hospital in Marburg

[1] This letter is printed in Klaus J. Heinisch, "Ein Brief Gregors IX an die hl. Elisabeth," *Franziskanische Studien* 25 (1938): 379-82, and Karl Wenck, "Die heilige Elisabeth und Papst Gregor IX," *Hochland* 5 (1907-1908): 129-47.

[2] The bull is published in A. Wyss, *Hessisches Urkendenbuch I. Urkundenbuch der Deutschordens-Ballei Hessen* (Leipzig, 1879), no. 18, pp. 16-17.

[3] Personnel at hospital; Huyskens, *Quellenstudien*, pp. 95-104.

[4] "Tochter Syon," in *Sanct Francisken Leben und Tochter Syon*, ed. Karl Weinhold (Paderborn: F. Schöningh, 1880), lines 50ff, pp. 322-23.

[5] What little is known about Gerard's life and his relationship to the mysticism of the time is discussed in the introduction to Karl Weinhold's edition of *Sanct Francisken Leben und Tochter Syon*, pp. 4-9, 17-18. For more about the figure of Lady Love or "Vrouwe Karitas," see Newman, *God and the Goddesses*, pp. 138-89; for Lamprecht's work, see especially pp. 158-59.

[6] For more on how the term *ancille* is used in the earliest sources, see Pieper, *St. Elizabeth of Hungary*, pp. 166-67.

[7] Pieper, "St. Elizabeth of Hungary and the Franciscan Tradition," p. 436.

Chapter XI: The Glory of Heaven

[1] Caesarius, "*Sermo de translatione B. Elizabete,*" no. 3; in Hilka, *Die Wundergeschichte*, p. 384.

[2] The translation here is mine. The document is also translated as "The Miracles List (1232)," in Wolf, *The Life and Afterlife of St. Elizabeth of Hungary*, pp. 83-90.

[3] From the introduction to the miracle accounts of 1233; see also the translation in Wolf, *Life and Afterlife*, p. 98. Because of manuscript variants, it is uncertain whether the text should read "ourselves" (*nos*), as Wolf reads, or "acquaintances" (*notos*), that is, acquaintances of Elizabeth. If the latter is true, it would mean that on that occasion other people than the four handmaids were questioned; the evidence of the Anonymous Franciscan seems to suggest this is so.

[4] No. 84 of the depositions on the miracles of 1233; Huyskens, *Quellenstudien*, p. 225; see also Wolf, *Life and Afterlife*, p. 154.

[5] Quoted in Ancelet-Hustache, *Gold Tried by Fire*, p. 133.

[6] These details come from a description of the canonization process attributed to the Dominican Raymond of Peñafort; "*Processus et ordo canonizationis beate Elyzabet,*" in Huyskens, *Quellenstudien*, pp. 145-46.

[7] Caesarius of Heisterbach, "*Sermo de translatione,*" no. 4, in Hilka *Wundergeschichte*, p. 386.

[8] Jean de Joinville, *Life of St. Louis*, Ch. XXI, par. 96 (Wailly ed).

[9] Biographical information about Blessed Gertrude is scarce. See Nesta de Robeck, *St. Elizabeth of Hungary: A Story of Twenty-four Years* (Milwaukee: Bruce Publishing Co., 1954), pp. 143-44. Much of her information, which I have relied on, is taken from an unpublished biography of Gertrude by Maria Helmers.

Chapter XII: Elizabeth's Legacy

[1] Raffaele Pazzelli, *The Franciscan Sisters: Outlines of History and Spirituality* (Steubenville, Ohio: Franciscan University, 1989), p. 20.

[2] Alfred Delp, S. J., "A Martyr's Voice," trans. and ed. by Lucia Simpson Shen, *America,* March 2, 1985, pp. 173-74.

Appendix: The Expulsion

[1] Huyskens, *Quellenstudien,* pp. 53-67.

[2] *Gold Tried by Fire*, p. 101.

[3] For a more complete discussion, see Lori Pieper, *St. Elizabeth of Hungary,* pp. 45-51 and 113-125.

Part II

Letter of Conrad of Marburg

[1] St. Raymond of Peñafort (ca. 1180-1275), a Dominican friar, who was called to Rome in 1230 to help codify the Church's canon law; he wrote works on penance and was also Pope Gregory IX's confessor.

[2] August 10, 1232.

[3] This might also be translated "in the presence of some of the brothers, she renounced her relative and children, her own will, all the pomps of the world," etc. We know from other sources that Conrad did ask Elizabeth to renounce her children.

[4] "To treat contraries by contraries" is a medical term dating back to Hippocrates. It refers to treatment of a disease with a medicine that produces the opposite effect (such as an anti-inflammatory drug to reduce inflammation). Hippocrates also

knew of the method of "treating similars by similars," which is the basis of homeopathic medicine. Here Elizabeth not only demonstrates her medical knowledge, but indicates that pride is a disease that must be cured by its opposite: humility.

[5] Most likely dysentery.

[6] Scabies is a skin disease caused by a mite that burrows under the skin to lay its eggs. It results in constant painful itching. Sulfur and borax were often used in the past to treat it.

[7] Cf. Luke 23:28.

[8] This last sentence is missing in some manuscripts, and may not be part of Conrad's original letter. Conrad's words above in the text indicate clearly that Elizabeth died during the night of November 16-17, 1231, and in fact, after midnight (at the first cockcrow), meaning her death took place on the 17th. This notice at the end, on the other hand, follows a medieval system of dating in which the day does not begin until sunrise, so by this reckoning, Elizabeth died on November 16.

Statements of the Four Handmaids

[1] The Italian mile was 5,000 feet, equivalent to the old Roman mile and more or less equivalent to our mile today (5,280 feet). The "long" German mile was five times this length.

[2] That is, her sister-in-law Jutta.

[3] Kitzingen am Main was a very old Benedictine monastery in Franconia; see Huyskens, *Quellenstudien*, p. 128 et passim.

[4] This is what some historians give as his correct name in Hungarian. The Latin text has "Pavias." See Ancelet Hustache, *Gold Tried by Fire*, pp. 182, 290.

[5] Huyskens believed that the town meant must actually be "Wetter." He noted that the town of Wehrda has no monastery, but that Elizabeth evidently did know Lutrude, the abbess of the

monastery in Wetter, who was present at her death; *Quellenstudien*, p. 131.

[6] Huykens believed that in this case as well the town meant must be Wetter, because unlike Wehrda, it had a magistrate of its own at this period; *Quellenstudien,* p. 134.

[7] Psalm 50, which begins: "Have mercy on me, O God."

Testimonies from the Anonymous Franciscan

[1] Malburg is a town in North Rhine-Westphalia.

[2] There are several places with the Latin name *Campania*, but the most likely one seems to be the town of Kempen in North Rhine-Westphalia.

[3] The author is anticipating a little here, because Gerard did not become minister of the Province of Upper Germany until around 1246, after Elizabeth's death. According to the lists studied by Konrad Eubel, OFM Conv, he was the fourth minister of the province; see his *Geschichte der oberdeutschen (Strassburger) Minoritenprovinz* (Wurzburg, 1886), pp. 157-59.

The Bull of Canonization

[1] Elizabeth actually died on November 17, 1231, as Conrad of Marburg's detailed account makes clear.

Bibliography

Sources for Elizabeth's Life

Only the main sources are listed here. All the passages quoted in the text are my translations from the original Latin, unless noted otherwise. I have also listed editions in English where available.

Arnaud de Serrant. "Chronica XXIV Generalium Ordinis Minorum." *Analecta Franciscana* 3 (Quaracchi, 1897).

Caesarius of Heisterbach. "Die Schriften des Caesarius von Heisterbach über die heilige Elisabeth von Thüringen." Ed. A. Huyskens, in A. Hilka ed., *Die Wundergeschichten des Caesarius von Heisterbach* (Bonn, 1937), 3:331-390.

"Cronica Reinhardsbrunnensis." ed. O. Holder-Egger, *Monumenta Germaniae Historica. Scriptores*, 30 (1896): 490-658.

Dietrich of Apolda. *Die Vita der heiligen Elisabeth des Dietrich von Apolda*. Ed. Monika Rener. Marburg: N. G. Elwert,

181

1993. (Veroffentlichen der Historischen Kommission für Hessen, 53).

Giordano of Giano. *Chronicle*. Translated in Placid Hermann, ed. *Thirteenth Century Chronicles*. Chicago: Franciscan Herald Press, 1961. The Latin text was edited in "Chronica Fratris Iordani." *Analecta Franciscana* 1 (1885): 1-19.

Glassberger, Nicholas. "De fratrum minorum ordinis origine eiusque progressu." *Analecta ad Fratrum Minorum Historiam* (Leipzig: Boehme, 1882), pp. 1-72.

Gregory IX, Pope. [Letter to Elizabeth]. Heinisch, Klaus J. "Ein Brief Gregors IX an die hl. Elisabeth." *Franziskanische Studien* 25 (1938): 379-82. Also edited in Wenck, Karl. "Die heilige Elisabeth und Papst Gregor IX." *Hochland* 5 (1907-1908): 129-47.

Huyskens, Albert. *Quellenstudien zur Geschichte der hl. Elisabeth, Landgrafin von Thüringen*. Marburg: N. G. Elwert, 1908. Contains editions of many of the documents of the canonization process, including the *Dicta*.

———. *Der sogennant Libellus de dictis quattuor ancillarum s. Elisabeth confectus*. Kempten und Munchen: Verlag der Jos. Kösel'schen Buchhandlung, 1911. An edition of the *Libellus* and discussion of the sources.

Pieper, Lori, SFO. "A New Life of St. Elizabeth of Hungary: The Anonymous Franciscan." Published in *Archivum Franciscanum Historicum* 93 (2000): 29-78. Description of the manuscripts and sources, followed by a complete edition of the Latin text. A revised version can be found in the Ph.D. dissertation below.

-----. "St. Elizabeth of Hungary and the Franciscan Tradition," Ph.d. Dissertation in history, Fordham University, New York, 2002, available on microfilm from UMI.

Posse, Otto, and Hubert Ermisch, eds. *Codex diplomaticus Saxoniae Regiae*. 1 Haupteil, III Band. Leipzig, 1898.

Santifaller, Leo. "Zur Originalüberlieferung der Heiligsprechungsurkunde der Landgrafin Elisabeth von Thüringen vom Jahre 1235." *Acht Jahrhunderte Deutscher Orden in Einzel-darstellungen*, ed. Klemens Wieser (Bad Godesburg: Verlag Wissenschafltliches Archiv, 1967), pp. 73-88.

Wolf, Kenneth Baxter. *The Life and Afterlife of St. Elizabeth of Hungary: Testimony From Her Canonization Hearings*. Oxford and New York: Oxford University Press, 2010. A good, readable translation of all the documents from the canonization process, with interpretative essays.

For Further Reading

These are a few of the most helpful books in English, though unfortunately most can be found only in libraries. For a much fuller bibliography covering works in all languages, see Pieper, *St. Elizabeth of Hungary, The Voice of a Medieval Woman*, pp. 230-50.

Ancelet-Hustache, Jeanne. *Gold Tried by Fire: St. Elizabeth of Hungary*. Chicago: Franciscan Herald Press, 1963. A excellent scholarly but readable biography, well documented, with extensive footnotes. The author describes Elizabeth's spiritual journey in detail. Some parts are a little outdated.

Coudenhove, Ida Friederike. *The Nature of Sanctity*. Tr. Ruth Bonsall and E. I. Watkin. London: Sheed and Ward, 1932. Not a biography, but a dialogue with an inquiring mind, it is a very readable, charming and fascinating study of Elizabeth's journey to sanctity.

Montalembert, Charles, comte de. *Life of St. Elizabeth of Hungary, Duchess of Thuringia*. There are a number of different English editions of this pioneer biography of St. Elizabeth, first published in French in 1836. It is not very rigorous in regard to understanding the comparative worth of the sources, but it really captures the medieval atmosphere through its many citations of the older legends, and gives a good idea of why people love Elizabeth.

Pieper, Lori, SFO. *St. Elizabeth of Hungary: The Voice of a Medieval Woman and Franciscan Penitent in the Sources for Her Life*. Loretto, PA: Franciscan Friars TOR, 2007. (A new edition is forthcoming). Studies the sources for Elizabeth's life in relation to each other, and examines the question of her Franciscan vocation in light of modern research on medieval women religious.

Robeck, Nesta De. *Saint Elizabeth of Hungary: A Story of Twenty- Four Years*. Milwaukee, Wisc.: Bruce Publishing Co, 1954. Another good biography in a popular style, with illustrations. Includes a partial (but rather faulty) English translation of some of the documents of the canonization process, the only one that has appeared in English until the publication of this book.

About the Author

Lori Pieper received her BA in the Humanities and MA in History from the University of Northern Iowa and her PhD in Medieval History from Fordham University, where she specialized in hagiography, Italian medieval history and women's religious history. Her other historical books include *St. Elizabeth of Hungary: The Voice of a Medieval Woman and Franciscan Penitent in the Sources for her Life* (2007). She has had articles published in many periodicals, including *Our Sunday Visitor*, *The Catholic Digest* and *L'Osservatore Romano*. She has also worked for some years as a professional translator. Since 1990, she has contributed translations of Pope John Paul I's writings to the journal *Humilitas*; some of these have appeared in *The Smiling Pope: The Life and Teaching of Pope John Paul I* (Our Sunday Visitor, 2004) and *A Passionate Adventure: Living the Catholic Faith Today* (Tau Cross Books and Media 2014). A member of the Secular Franciscan Order, she lives and works in the Bronx, New York.

Available from Tau Cross Books and Media:

A Woman for Our Time: St. Elizabeth of Hungary (DVD)

A Passionate Adventure: Living the Catholic Faith Today by Pope John Paul I (e-book and paperback)

The Greatest of These is Love: The Life of St. Elizabeth of Hungary (2nd rev ed) by Lori Pieper (e-book and paperback).

www.taucrossbooks.com

Tau Cross Books and Media
30 W. 190th St., Apt. 6N
Bronx, NY 10468-2553
(646) 938-0432

CPSIA information can be obtained
at www.ICGtesting.com
Printed in the USA
LVHW02s0839220818
587247LV00002B/126/P